The Pearl of Sufism

Seyed Mostafa Azmayesh

Mehraby Publishing House

First Edition was published in the United Kingdom in 2008 by Mehraby Publication.

Copyright © 2008 English translation printed by Mehraby Publishing House

mehrabbyfoundation@yahoo.com

Copyright © 2008/16 by Dr S M Azmayesh

2nd Edition 2016.

ISBN 978-0-9935347-2-0

All rights reserved

No part of this book may be reproduced or utilised in any form or by any means, electronic or mechanical, without the written permission of the *Publisher*

Contents

Preface 5

Introduction 11

Chapter 1: Sheikh Kamel 19

Chapter 2: The Qanat 29

Chapter 3: The rhythms and the poetry 39

Chapter 4: Time and events 53

Chapter 5: The relation with the Master 63

Chapter 6: Fanaticism 81

Chapter 7: One Letter 91

Chapter 8: Jesus and Barnabas 101

Chapter 9: The Pearl 121

Chapter 10: Warnings 141

Chapter 11: Rumi and Shams 153

Chapter 12: Aphorisms 171

Chapter 13: A brief history of Sufism 181

Acknowledgements 197

Preface

There are many books about Islamic mysticism and Sufism. In most cases these are books about ancient Sufi masters like Rumi and Hafez. But a book written by a contemporary Sufi master is rare. This is a book by Seyed Mostafa Azmayesh, the official representative of the Nematollah Gonabadi Sufi Order in the West. He writes penetratingly about the 'Path of the Substantial Evolution'. But Seyed Mostafa Azmayesh is not only a Sufi master, he is also a researcher. He graduated at the Sorbonne (Paris) on the subject of Islamic Gnosis; an ideal combination: mystic and scientific researcher. In fact it is the only good combination, because the true mystic is a scientific researcher. A scientist of the soul, a scientist of the spirit.

Like a chemist who researches and works with matter, the mystic investigates and works in the inner laboratory. A mystic is an alchemist; he perceives how the 'substance of the soul' changes as he approaches God. In this book, the inner changes are precisely described; the negation, the temptation, the destruction, the acceptance, the ascendance and the liberation and in the end, the surrendering to God. These are the stages on the path of 'Substantial Development', a journey which starts with the ego and ends in God.

The path that changes leads into gold. In this book, Seyed Mostafa Azmayesh emphasises again and again that this 'Path of Substantial Development' is no easy path to travel. It needs a great deal of discipline. Because of this, it is better not to travel alone even if the path could be travelled alone. The serious seeker needs a master. In the West, we have lost to a great extent the sense of importance of a spiritual teacher. It has a negative connotation: a Master... That is something from the East! We in the West are our own spiritual Master; at least, this is what we think. And so – we can assume – spiritual growth in the West is superficial.

Seyed Azmayesh says: 'The Master chooses against the ego'. In the West, we choose by our ego. And so, we spiritually 'shop around', as long as our ego is satisfied. Seyed Azmayesh, however, explains very clearly in this book that you need a Master on this path. The Master helps us to dominate our ego in order that the 'higher self' can come in control. The Master knows the dangers on the path of transition to one's substance. He prevents us, he stimulates us, he puts you in front of situations and most of all he gives us love. Therefore it is good advice to follow a Master, even though you yourself do not know why – not yet.

To follow does not mean to abandon one's own will: it is the student who chooses the Master, it is the student decides whom he obeys and to whom 'he falls in love'. The true Master teaches in parts, he gives to the student what the student can digest and not more! The Master is connected to God; the seeker is mainly connected to his ego at the start. The stories are numerous - also in this book- in which the student starts out to find his Master. Not the other way round!

In the understanding of Islam, Jesus was not crucified. However, according to Christianity he was. So there is a problem! At least, there is a problem in theology, not for the mystic. Because, crucified or not, it is important that Jesus has returned. For the Islamic and the Christian mystics that is the focus. 'The seeker always awaits the coming of Christ in his heart', writes Azmayesh. Jesus is always there, the mystic, also the Islamic mystic, is able to experience Jesus. And more, it is the goal of Islamic mysticism to experience Jesus within their hearts. Only when you know Jesus in your heart, can you recognise Jesus in the outer world. How? By observing other people. 'When you see Christ in your heart, He brings you peace and quietness and when you meet somebody who gives you this feeling you have met Christ'. In another human being! Within Sufism, Jesus is the true Master.

This is no surprise because Seyed Azmayesh shows in this book that Sufism is older than the Islam and it has its roots within Gnosticism and Christian mysticism. So, the final goal of Christian mysticism and Islamic mysticism is the same: to find Jesus within the heart. The trans-substantial stages of the soul are also the same. The mystical techniques differ greatly with (medieval) Christian mysticism. In Christian mysticism the techniques are more cerebral, while the methods of Islamic mysticism are artful in the first place. The different techniques are precisely described in this book. Like the rhythms that are 'hidden' within the mystical poetry of Rumi for example.

The reciting of the mystical poetry, called Qawwal, brings the heart in tune with the inner development. Also the Quran is filled with rhythms. Reciting the verses of the Quran changes the rhythm of the heart. For the Sufis, the Quran is more a book of recitations than it is a theological book. To the Sufis, Mohammad is more a mystic than a founder of a religion. Often the recitations are supported and accompanied by rhythmical music, like the playing of the Daf[1]. Like in the old Western music, Gregorian chanting is meant to bring the body in tune with the divine rhythm.

Another important technique is the telling of stories, by which your head becomes your heart. For this reason stories have been included within this book. All these techniques are meant to bring the heart in tune with the divine rhythm.

Of course the changes cannot be perceived by the naked eye, these are subtle changes which can only be noticed by the spiritual eye and ear. The Master can hear them; and God who hears in the attuned rhythms an invitation to enter inside.

Dr. John van Schaik.

(John van Schaik (1956) studied medieval Mysticism and Gnosticism at the University of Utrecht and the University of Antwerp. He did his PhD at the Catholic University of Nijmegen on a comparative Study of Dualism among the Manicheans and Cathars. He is co-founder and Director of the Origenes Institute in the Netherlands. The Origenes Institute is specialised in the relationship between esoteric Christianity and the established Church. He is also editorial chief of BRES, a review on religion, science and gnosis. He has published widely in the field of esoteric Christianity).

---

[1] Daf is a Persian hand drum.

Figure 1 - Baptism (or Initiation) of Jesus by St John the Baptist

Introduction

'Once, Alexander the Great and his army were in search of the source of life. During the night they were travelling, they felt little rocky pieces beneath their feet. Some of them collected a few of these things; some of them ignored these stony things. When the light appeared the next day all of them cried out. During the night some of them had collected what now appeared to be jewels and the ones who had not bothered to collect something cried because they were empty-handed. The ones who had collected something cried because they had only collected such a small amount. In this story, jewels are the symbol of time...'

When we look at the sky during a bright night it is filled with stars. We experience feelings of awe, beauty and astonishment when we look at this silent universe. In most cases we don't realise that by looking at the stars, in fact we are looking back in time. In some cases the starlight we see has been radiated from the stars decades ago, but the light of most of the stars we see, has travelled thousands or millions of years before falling on our eyes. At the same time, we see a multitude of stars in the same moment. This is the paradox of time.

The oldest light that has been captured by science until now is over 13 billion years old. The starlight tells us about the birth of this visible universe. According to the scientists this universe emerged from a very small particle and before this there was 'nothing'. Much from what has come into existence by this big bang we can experience with our senses. But the universe we live in must have an origin, a creator.

According to the Sufis, the creator was 'like a hidden treasure that wanted to be known'. From this sentence follows that there must be a creator, a creation and something, or someone, who is able to know and to understand this treasure. An image of a triangle appears before us, a triangle formed by the creator, the creation and mankind.

Knowing and understanding the creation is the challenge and the task that we are facing. This is the crucial point in which we differ from the rest of nature, including the animals. A deer for instance sees the flowing water in the river, but only a human being understands that this water must have come from somewhere and goes somewhere else. This realisation brings a big responsibility, not just a passive responsibility that goes as far as just taking notice of the events that happen, but an active responsibility.

In fact we are able to distinguish between different forces and energies and we are also able to re-shape and re-create these forces. It is here that we find the goal of Sufism. In the Path of the Substantial Evolution[2] I change my inner forces by gaining more and more the control over my ego. I start to develop my hidden capacities. The goal is to eliminate duality and establish unity. The secret of unity lies in the rhythms, but that is getting ahead of ourselves.

---

[2] The path of Substantial Evolution is a method of spiritual development that transforms a human-animal to a complete human being and beyond. Moreover, it's a path that develops the hidden capacities of the soul that all human being possess.

Introduction

Mankind, when developed to its full potential, has the function of being the eyes of the universe. The Creator manifests himself constantly, in every second; and mankind is needed to experience this process. Sufism regards every aspect and everything in the universe as a different name of God, the Creator. Our heartbeat constantly repeats the name of our Creator. To travel to this core requires a method, a balanced system of appropriate exercises; in other words it requires a school.

Sufism is not a religion, neither a description of life to be memorised, nor is it is a system of laws that can be imposed on us, and it's not a sect and no '*ism*'.

Sufism is a path, an art, a way of life that demands determination, trust, endurance and patience of the student. First you are attracted, gradually you want to know more and in the end it is rooted in your life so deeply that you want to be a disciple. The word 'disciple' is derived from the word 'discipline', meaning that it is not without engagement; if you want to reach to the centre of yourself, to your essence, you will have to make the journey in the depths of yourself.

In order to travel on this path you have to be well-equipped and well-trained. On top of this, the road leads through dark and unknown territory; you need to secure for yourself the help of a faithful guide. Sufism is a path, a method.

For instance you can compare it with learning the Chinese language. There are, of course, different methods to study Chinese. First, as a student I have to find out which method suits me the best and after this I have to go in search of a school in which this method is being taught. I have to register and maybe I have to take an exam before I am allowed to start the classes. Or maybe I will have to follow another course first. Then, the day comes when I receive my application forms and after I have signed them I get an identification card that proves that I am registered. However, when I just put this card in my pocket it does not help me to learn the Chinese language. When I don't attend the lessons, I learn nothing.

Sufism is a school that has certain ceremonies at certain times. In some cases, people think that by just attending the ceremonies one is a Sufi, but this is not the case; all the ceremonies and folklore are secondary.

When I really want to learn something, I need to be motivated and seriously determined to reach my goal. Then it depends on the methods that are applied, the capacities of the teacher and my own capacities. For instance, I want to study music and I have the capacity for it, but if I then go to a school in order to learn to paint, it would be a waste of time. On the other hand, if I am talented in painting I won't see much result from music lessons, even with the best teachers.

When you make a choice you have to consider four things; the truth of the school, your own capacities, the capacities of the teachers and your own will.

When you hear Chinese people talk to each other, it can become the reason that you want to learn their language, but once you have started out at school it may prove to be harder than you had thought. Your will is needed to learn things gradually.

The will has to team up with patience. Patience is the will to continue until the end. You may be very enthusiastic and you start fast. After two years you conclude that this was not what you were looking for.

These reasons demonstrate why it is very important to investigate the four points mentioned above before starting on the path. In reality much work has to be done before even embarking on the path. Before you choose a school, you have to be very critical and verify everything thoroughly because when you start badly prepared, conflicts easily happen, not only conflicts within yourself, but also conflicts with others, which creates a negative atmosphere around you. Of course, when you set off on the path you will be confronted as you go. This is why you need to be sure about your choice and eliminate the problems you have within yourself before you start.

You can compare it with the decision to marry somebody. You figure out before whether you really want to marry this person because afterwards you will be facing all kinds of situations and problems together. So, when you already have certain problems within yourself, this will make the situation more complicated. Look and investigate critically, in a positive way. If you don't have the will to continue till the end, it is better not to start at all. By refraining from it you avoid problems for everybody.

When you enter the path you can compare it to a journey by boat. You start out and during the travel you can be dissatisfied with the boat or have a lot of comments for the captain. But in fact you will have little choice. There's no alternative, but to jump from the ship.

> *On a hot day, a Master took his students out to a field. The land was dry and it was clear that it needed to be irrigated in order to be fruitful. Spread*

out over the land there were five wells and the owner of the land was busy digging a sixth hole.

None of the holes were made deep enough to contain water. "Look" the Master said, "Several times this farmer has changed his mind about the best spot to dig a well and every time he started out he stopped after a while. Had he been determined he certainly would have had one well deep enough to contain water. Now he is still without water and also his land is wasted."

Sufism is a school where you can develop your hidden capacities, capacities which cannot be developed by your parents and which are not taught in the regular schools. Sufism can, so to speak, be seen as complementary to regular education. Most people however, don't see any reason to do so, especially not when it requires a long study under the guidance of a teacher.

When you develop and grow by going on the path you discover different aspects of love. You meet other creatures and there can be a lot of other discoveries. Those aspects are not the goal. The goal is to know yourself.

You can compare it to planting a small seed in the earth. Much work will have to be done in darkness, apparently without quick results. In the end, a tree will grow which will yield fruit.

As Sufism is described here it seems like a rational method which urges the student to learn about himself by experience. However, it cannot be compared to a straight road leading from 'A' to 'B'. As described before, it is an individual path. Moreover the Master will, instead of presenting an answer or a solution, confront the student with the jungle of life and place him in the midst of a multitude of possibilities in order to find out his own way.

An important aspect of Sufism is that the student lives in the society often with obligations like being a parent, having a job and other social responsibilities; in the midst of everyday life the student finds his way.

Let's describe it through an image: first, the path leads the seeker through a jungle filled with dangerous animals like dinosaurs and tigers. When he becomes more advanced, he will be in a wood surrounded by noble animals like horses and deer. Eventually he will reach a heaven; garden with all kinds of birds.

Sufism is the way of the heart, a method: come in contact with our 'Substantial Being' by means of our heart and gradually have extra sensorial perceptions as to how to know a universe that is only accessible by extra sensorial perception.

This method has nothing to do with psychoanalysis, the unconscious, spiritual therapy or other methods like activating chakras, shamanism or acupuncture. Without judging these methods, it needs to be stressed that mixing this method with other methods or adjusting it to your own desires can be dangerous and does not yield results.

Within this method the student aims towards the future. Instead of treating and examining all kind of problems from the past, the student gradually discovers his own creative powers.

Because the path is individual and different for each of us, a book can only partially describe it. Everyone who seriously wants to learn shall be taught collectively, but also individually. At same time, in our present state each one of us perceives reality in a different way. A story that is being told evokes different reactions in each one of us and it can even be so when the reader has put the book away for a year and afterwards reads it again, other thoughts and new impressions will arise.

In the different chapters we will try to describe different aspects of the mystical journey. As in the previous book, Teachings of a Sufi Master, we sit down at the feet of Sheikh Kamel and listen. With warmth and wisdom he explains many facets of the jewel that is called Sufism.

There will be many subjects and some parts of the book leave a strong impression. Often there will be examples and stories. The last ones appeal to a different part of our brain than theoretical language appeals to. Stories stimulate the faculty of imagination, the faculty which is so important in Sufism.

The two last chapters, containing aphorisms and the history of Sufism, can be seen as complementary. We want to conclude with a practical point.

In Sufism women and men are regarded as equal, having exactly the same potential. For practical reasons the Master and student are described throughout this book as 'he', but this term applies to both sexes. Many facts about women in mystical history has often been deliberately ignored and forgotten. So, we often will unveil historical examples of men, as well as some surprising facts about women mystics, fully conscious of the fact that women and men are equal.

Chapter 1: Sheikh Kamel

The students sit on their cushions. Apart from some soft sounds the chapel is silent. Sunlight shines through the stained glass windows and the singing of the birds makes the silence almost tangible. Most of the students subscribed themselves for being here for one week. They all have arranged their life in order to be at the retreat site for a week. All have come for Sheikh Kamel. Most of them have spent more time at workshops with Sheikh Kamel, while some of them have seen the Sheikh only during one lecture and now want to find out more. Everyone has subscribed to a programme, which includes the lectures of Sheikh Kamel, practising on the Daf, the Persian frame-drum, calligraphy, meditation and actively supporting the programme in a practical way in and around the house.

In a small room downstairs, Sheikh Kamel will stay during the week. He is connected to the students unable to attend the workshop by phone and by internet. From behind his small desk he is in contact with other students who are involved in a number of other projects. He also sleeps here for just a few hours each night and he eats here, also students can have an individual talk with him here. He broadcasts his radio programmes from this room and he uses it to pray and to study.

Softly the door of the chapel opens and Sheik Kamel enters. He walks to the front, sits and takes out his Tasbi (a type of rosary made from the string of beads that is used to pray). With his eyes and some physical gestures he greets his students before starting to talk.

"Sufism is not a religion, nor a sect. It is not an 'ism'. Sufism is the art of love; it is the way to self-consciousness. Self-consciousness is the shortest way to understand the universe. It is the shortest way to understand the relation between the Creator and the creation.

The universe has been created naturally, according to natural and harmonious laws. Stars and other celestial bodies move in harmonious and fixed ways and the whole universe functions according to the same laws.

How are we able to understand these laws? The law of gravity for instance is a universal that is valid in the whole universe. When we strike out to learn more about this law, we investigate how the stars turn and how the planets rotate around their sun. The shortest, easiest and most direct way, however, is to try to understand how an apple falls from a tree. When you understand this, you understand how this law functions in the whole universe.

Sufism is the path of emptiness and in order to understand this mystery we listen to lamenting song of the reed flute, the Ney. A Sufi tries to understand himself. When he understands himself, he understands the whole universe.

The central question is: "Who am I?" By only posing the question you will fail to get an answer. It just confuses you; your mind will come up with a standard answer or flood your consciousness with associations and thoughts, which make you forget the initial question. How are you able to find a substantial answer to this question? It can only be done by applying a method, the method of negation. This method of negation is used by the Sufis to penetrate deeper and deeper into this question. This is done by posing the question: "What am I?" Every moment I have experiences and with each experience I ask: "Am I this?" "Am I my name? Am I my job? Am I my social life? Am I the clothes I wear? Am I the image that others have of me? Am I my thoughts, my feelings? Am I my body? Am I the image of myself which I see in the mirror?"

This is an intensive process, a long and arduous exercise. When we want to have a small quantity of perfume, when we want to distil a small quantity of essence, we need a huge amount of petals. The remaining extract, the perfume, we call the substance. In the process of distilling the perfume we purify it from everything which it is not, we remove the skins and the dust until the pure perfume remains. The process takes place under great pressure.

The same route is taken in order to find diamonds. Before reaching to the diamonds, first we have to remove tons of stones and carbon. We have to remove everything which is not a diamond. When you are in the middle of the desert and you are thirsty, what will you do?

You dig a well to the water, in other words, you remove everything that is not water. This is the Path of the Substantial Evolution.

In other words, consider your true self as being like Nabat. Nabat (crystal of sugar) cannot crystallise without first being dissolved in water. So, for crystallisation to occur, the sugar has to be dissolved in the water. The water is the reality, the intervention of the Master, in order to allow this process to occur. We have to accept certain psychological conditions. This process of dissolution is called Fana in Sufism, which means annihilation. The sugar is completely dissolved, but it is only when it has disappeared completely that it can crystallise. Crystallisation in Sufism is called Baqa, which means to become eternal."

Sheikh Kamel pauses for a while to look around. "During a clear night you are able to see about 3,000 stars with the naked eye. Imagine that you take a picture of the whole night. However, instead of using a camera which captures just a single moment, you expose the film for the entire duration of the night.

When you look at the picture that you develop you will see that it consists of thousands of white circles. When we look at the stars at night it appears that they have fixed places. Because of the rotation of the earth around its axis; however, it will look like the stars make a circle. There remains one star in your picture that does not make a circle. This is the polestar; it is in line with the axis of the earth. The polestar has fascinated people for thousands of years. In periods of migration often there were groups of people who went in search of the polestar. For a Sufi, it is the same; he is only interested in his inner polestar.

Everyone has this fixed point within himself. If we thoroughly study everything around us we have to conclude that everything around us is in movement. These movements can be obvious or hardly recognisable yet, all is in movement. Mystics have always been in search of the fixed point within themselves. The Path of the Substantial Development is this migration, the journey from me to *me*. During the journey, I abandon my false self. It is the journey leading from self-denying to self-consciousness.

The starting point and the goal, the subject and object are fixed. To put it in other words, I travel from me to me, in me and by me. I am the point of departure; I am the goal, the journey and the traveller. This path of self-knowledge can be compared to the method of the French philosopher Descartes.

Descartes started to doubt everything until he finally reached a point that could not be denied anymore. He described his discovery as 'I think, therefore I am'. Years before Descartes wrote about it, this path had been discovered by Avicenna, a Sufi mystic whose book about these subjects had been reprinted several times.

This fixed point that is talked about is the solid base. It is in you and in me. This touchstone, this substantial point within me, is the point that in the end cannot be denied anymore, the point that cannot be put away. The specific and unique feature of this point is that it is self-conscious. It does not take itself as something else; it does not identify itself with something else and therefore never makes a mistake.

The moment you realise the presence of this essential substance the first part of the journey, the period of asking and denying is over. The second journey begins with the question how we can develop this inner substance. From this question immediately one asks which method has to be applied for this development.

You have to realise that, before you have finished the first journey, all the ideas and concepts that you have about God are not rooted within your real self. The most important lesson of the first journey is that we have to know ourselves before we can know God. Before having finished the first journey statements of 'being with' or 'being without God' are an illusion.

Some people identify themselves with a certain part of the material world: a house, a career... Others have money as their illusion and some have God as their illusion. When you know yourself, you know God; this is the foundation of Sufism.

The one who starts the search tries to understand himself. He tries to do this by removing everything that he is not. This is the process of denial. Sufism is the path of poverty, the path of emptiness. A Sufi is often compared to a reed flute, a Ney. The Ney has been cut from its origin and it longs to go back to it. Its origin is the country of nothing. The land of nothing is filled with the light of God and it is so fulfilled that there is no place for illusions.

The Sufi looks for the substantial *Me* by putting away everything that it is not. When the inner substance is discovered, the seeker notices that this inner substance of Me is the same as your inner substance and the inner substance of everybody. Then there is the realisation of unity. To be separated is an illusion.

When several people each dig a well, everybody sees the same sun reflected at the bottom. In order to find the sun you need to be poor, humble, nothing. Each well has the shape of a flute and it is filled with emptiness. From every well sounds the same melody of water, life and love. The NeyFlute is the canal. It is not a canal for air but a canal for fire – the energy of the heart. The Ney tells the story of love, the tale of longing and nostalgia".

Sheikh Kamel nods when one of his students wants to pose a question.

"What is the significance of being separated from our origin?"

He answers, "The goal is to learn to know and to understand ourselves, to learn to know who I am. Every one of us is like an oyster with the possibility to create a pearl. Still, many oysters are empty because not many people feel the need to create a pearl.

Our inner substance is like a small seed, a tiny seed which can sprout into a huge cypress tree: it is like an egg that can grow into a huge bird. It is important that I consider myself as a tiny seed. After this I have to do the utmost to develop this immense power. The travellers on this path have to pay attention to their heart not to their head. So they try to be aware of their heartbeat. This inner journey, by means of the rhythms, is a musical journey."

Another student poses a question: "When the oyster is empty and it is satisfied with this, isn't this exactly the purpose we have?"

Sheikh Kamel looks at the woman who has posed the question: "There are two kinds of blackness. First there is darkness by which we mean the absence of light. Secondly, there is the colour black, the colour in which all other colours have merged. The seven colours of the spectrum together generate the colour black. The journey we make leads us from ignorance to self-consciousness. The fact that the oyster is empty is due to its ignorance. It is poor on the inside since its attention is constantly oriented outwards. By applying the principle of negation we finally arrive inside ourselves.

Then there's the situation of inner richness and outer poorness. When I am outwardly rich and inwardly poor, I must try to change my habits in order to develop my inner side and to become poor on the outside. The journey is made through the rhythms. In fact, the seeker makes four journeys.

During the first journey he denies everything that is not his inner substance. By this method he or she learns to know his inner substance. The second journey is the development of this inner substance. This part of the complete journey can be compared to descending into a very deep well. During the third part of the journey the seeker shows the way to others. Here the seeking stops and giving the education starts. The fourth stage of the journey is being in the presence of every seeker until they have completed their journey.

The ultimate goal of the journey is not to become self-conscious; this is only the first step.

The goal is a state in which we are completely immersed and intoxicated by love. Without being conscious of myself I cannot fall in love. First the Master breaks our ego, and then he makes us drunk.

In all four parts of the journey you work with the rhythms. The rhythms you receive from your teacher. Every rhythm, every melody is like a bridge to the heartbeat; when you play a certain rhythm for two minutes, your mental and your spiritual state change.

A part of a mystical poem is called Beit, which means 'house'. Every house has an owner. The owner is the inner vibration. The fact that the poem has a meaning is not the most important part of it. Giving meaning to a poem by the use of words is only the pretext to create the poem. The power is in the inner vibration.

It is clear that the meaning of the words only can be understood by persons who speak the same language. The inner vibration is experienced by everyone. The inner vibration works in the heart of every living creature with a heart."

There is another question: "Can the mystical poems, like the ones from the Masnavi be translated correctly?"

"Every poem describes a poet's spiritual experience. You have to be in the same state as the poet to fully understand the poem. A literal translation only displays a superficial meaning. It is like wanting to encompass the ocean by glancing at the froth and the waves – all you see is the foam of the surface. The true meaning lies hidden on the bottom like a pearl. The Pir, the Master, is like a staircase to heaven. Think of an arrow and a bow: The seeker is like the arrow, the Pir is like the bow that gives the energy to the arrow. The rhythms provide the energy to rise up from the physical, the astral, the mental and the energetic bodies.

The Master is playing Rumi like a musical instrument, from every particle of your existence this rhythm raises. Rumi did not become the instrument, he became the vibration. The end of the journey is to be this vibration to realise the unity of the visible and invisible world."

After a short silence Sheikh Kamel starts reciting.

Chapter 2: The Qanat

It is silent in the chapel, yet all the students have gathered and are waiting for Sheikh Kamel. The door opens and he enters. When he sits he holds his rosary, remaining silent for a few minutes. Then he looks up.

"On the path of Sufism we move in the direction of the mystery. We engage in the mystery of our life. This mystery is something we do not understand. There is something that calls us and slowly a great longing arises to name this mystery, to experience it and to go in search of it. When we do not understand this mystery and still try to explain it, then it becomes superstition. The understanding of the mystery, the demystification can be realised only by digging a canal within us.

In fact there are three ways to penetrate into a mystery. In the first place we have, in common with animals, our instinct. Secondly, common to machines and animals, we can make use of our reason.

Thirdly, we can approach a mystery with our heart. Our reason and instinct are located within our brain and spirituality is located within our heart. You should note that we need our reason in order to communicate about the mystery.

The mystery which we want to approach is made up of two parts, a causal part that falls under the laws of cause and effect, and a part which follows the laws of synchronicity. By our reason we can only understand the causal part and so, we will never be able to grasp the whole mystery by our reason.

Our reason, when we use it in a proper way, works in four steps. First I think how something might function. After this, I make a hypothesis of this. Then I go and test the hypothesis and by the results I generate a law. This law can be applied in the world around me.

Religious leaders do not follow their heart. They only reason about questions; then by thinking, arguing and building systems, they try to explain the mystery. Sects and cults, which also have the mystery as their main subject, try to keep it secret and obscure. Often they apply a secret language or they have initial degrees that need to be obtained. In contradiction to the theological approach and the approach of the sects and the cults, Sufism tries to explain the mystery by penetrating it.

The way the Sufi travels in order to solve the mystery is the way from the head to the heart. The first step on the Path of the Substantial Evolution is to learn to listen to your heartbeat. In order to experience our heartbeat, our head has to be empty, without thoughts. How can we go from our head to our heart? Our whole life we are used to trust on our five senses and these five senses keep us tightly connected to the material world."

The story of an old man

The Kabootar-Khan Lake is situated sixty-five kilometres westward of the Iranian city of Kerman in the south of Iran. It stretches over five acres with an average depth of six metres and it has emerged through the construction of a dam. This whole irrigation system has been created by only one man, named Haj Hossein Hassani who began working on it in 1979. Now after twenty-five years, the surrounding areas are overgrown with tamarisk bushes and the lake has become a place for migratory birds. Probably this is the youngest lake in Iran, and in its presence the view of the sunset fills the onlooker with awe and joy.

The practical work of just one man has resulted in this beautiful place. Without scientific or financial support, he has created this wonderful lake relying solely on his experience of the environment.

So we listen to this 80 year old powerful, determined man who has created, in one of the driest and saltiest environments, a place that evokes admiration. His eyes sparkle and his skin is tanned by years of hard labour, yet his face shows determination. He tells us that after the revolution he started this project by making canals and dams. At first people thought he was crazy, but after long years when the project began to reach its conclusion they became more respectful. He describes how he had built a fourteen kilometre canal from the river so that when the river flooded, the lake would fill with water.

In the first year water flowed into the lake and he made a basin to capture it. Slowly, after many years the lake began to expand.

He is very happy with the results of his work and while offering his guests refreshments he says: "This is the way of Aly. Aly gave us the example how to deal with the wolves at our doorstep. The ones who truly want to call themselves seekers on the path, should plant a tree or realise something that leaves the world a bit more beautiful, instead of being indifferent."

Sheikh Kamel drinks from his tea; the story has made a tangible impression.

He continues: "The material world in which we live can be compared to a desert. Everyone is thirsty and a lot of people are in search of water. The surface of the desert is constantly changing because of storms and shifting sands. The only thing the desert can offer is the illusion of water. The little bit of water we find in the desert is salty and not fit to quench our thirst. Often we think we see an oasis at the horizon, but when we get nearer it is a mirage, an illusion.

Desperately we want to know how we can get to the life-giving source of water. The water is deeply beneath our feet, originating from the heart of the mountain. However, we need to construct an underground canal to reach it.

The builder of the Qanat (underground canal) is called a 'Moganny'. He constructs an irrigation system in order for the water to flow beneath the ground to the middle of the desert.

The seeker digs a hole in the darkness to make contact with the water. However, the water is 72,000 metres away in the mountain. The work starts in the middle of the desert without any point of orientation, and leads to the reserve of water that is stored in darkness. How does the seeker know that he is digging in the right direction?

A seeker longs for God, his intentions are pure.

A good attitude and a goal are important. Every moment you have to be willing to alter your direction. When you make a deviation of ten centimetres in the beginning, in the end you miss your goal by ten kilometres! Because, you are no longer conscious of the fact that you are diverted from your goal.

A sea turtle comes to the land in order to lay her eggs hundred meters from the coast, in the warm sand. Then she returns to the ocean while the sun and the sand create the conditions for the baby turtle to grow inside the egg. The baby turtle crawls out of the egg and finds his way to the ocean on his own. It is trusting to its sixth sense. When it is crawling towards the sea the heartbeat is at a steady pace. But when it deviates from its goal, the heartbeat becomes uneasy. In this way it reaches the ocean.

The seeker who digs the canal is oriented on his heartbeat. In this way the Master is the best friend of the student. Of course he is much more than that and it would be a mistake of the student to consider the Master just a friend. The student is not able to correct his course by himself.

Only with the help of the Master he is able to fight his desires in a proper way. Acceptance and discipline are the key words. The student who makes the canal is oriented around his heart; it has nothing to do with the head. It is not only that the canal has to be constructed, it also has to be kept clean. The cleaning of the canal and keeping it empty is done by discipline, self-criticism and service. Every student only keeps his attention on his own canal.

All the deserts are protected by mountains. These high mountains capture the roaming clouds. The mountain is the barrier between the material world and the multi-dimensional world. Every desert is bordered and protected by a mountain, its peak rising above the clouds, its roots deep in the earth. The mountain always wears a white cap. Alexander the Great was astonished when he approached the mountain Qaf. The mountain Qaf said: "I have my canals to all mountains and cities". On top of the mountain lives the Simorg, a royal bird. And he teaches his children.

When we are looking for water we have to bow down. We need to become humble. Only emptiness, humble and low, can receive the water. Our heart is composed of more than sixty-five percent water; and in listening to our heartbeat; we are listening to the divinity. During your journey in the darkness you are being guided by your heartbeat, your sixth sense. The master reminds us that the material world is empty, that it is an illusion. Life does not spring from the desert, it comes from another place. Life comes from the mountain; the mountain is the source of eternal life.

The construction of an irrigation system is a collective work. In the desert seven groups of people live and there are seven fields. The eighth field is invisible. Everyone is responsible for his own development, but we are connected to each other. A horizontal canal is constructed from the centre of the desert to the heart of the mountain. But in order to have a constant flow of water, it is necessary to dig vertical wells every five metres. The Qanat is a system of irrigation, made of a small horizontal tunnel with vertical shafts that make the water flow. Even today, this system is found in many regions in Iran. It is a very vulnerable system, because when one of the vertical wells gets blocked, the water stops running.

The metaphor of the Qanat symbolises the science of inner development. The water brings life to the desert. This life bringing water comes to the middle of the desert by an underground canal. The water that falls on the slopes of the mountains and the hills gets dirty as it brings down a lot of sand and stones. When this water reaches the desert, it is polluted. In contrast, the pure and clean water comes from an underground system. And one should be aware that heavy rainfall and floods are dangerous and harmful for the Qanat.

The mountain, the desert and the clouds form a complete ecological system. A Sufi looks for the emptiness of the desert and each desert is protected by a mountain. Each mountain is, in its turn, a canal from the mountain Qaf.

Mountain Qaf is the border between this and the other world. The soul is like a bird that lands on the mountain. And, as this story clearly shows, in the material world from where there is a possibility to make contact with the other world. The door to this world is in the heart.

As we said there are seven regions in the desert, seven villages, and seven fields. Each village gets water from the Qanat, one day of the week. The people of all the villages, of the whole area are responsible for the maintenance of the Qanat. Each one has to be constantly alert in order to keep the water flowing. The water is spread out in a natural way. When you live in the desert you are under the influence of all kinds of circumstances and changes. There will be good moments as well as bad moments. Being in contact with the stream of the Qanat gives you harmony and peace.

A regular heartbeat orients us in the right direction and the *Zekr* [3]brings harmony to your heart and keeps you on the good path. The heart of a Sufi functions as a compass. Everyone is responsible for his own part of the Qanat and at the same time we are

---

[3] Zekr is a type of mantra based on the names of God. A more detail explanation of different types of Zekr can be found in The Teachings of A Sufi Master - S.M Azmayesh, Mehraby Publication, 2nd Edition, 2016.

interconnected. Sometimes this becomes clear when you ask a question and immediately you feel the answer. This is why you sometimes pose the question of another person. Together we are responsible for the whole system. The method we use to dig and maintain the canal is the method of the rhythms and the poetry."

It is silent in the chapel and after some minutes Sheikh Kamel starts to recite.

"When we think of the universe

See that everything moves

The biggest and the smallest

We are not more important than the smallest particle

We can also reach the sun

Everything is in movement following the universal love

All motion is in perfect harmony

Everything dances to an inner music

So God is the composer and the musician."

The Qanat

Figure 2- A Sufi Sama gathering[4]

---
[4] Public domain picture (1892) https://archive.org/details/popularsciencemo41newy

Chapter 3: The rhythms and the poetry

Sheikh Kamel pauses for the inner vibration of his recitation to take effect on the heart and the mind of his students and then he gently looks up and says:

"Sufism is the school of the substantial evolution. What is meant by substantial evolution?" We mean by this the transformation of all subatomic particles of the sun, to the light – perhaps this sounds very abstract and scientific to your ears. If we put it differently, we can say that Sufism is based on silence and listening to the inner music. The goal of the seeker is to become one, to unite with this inner music. How can this transformation be realised?

On this path we work on this transformation through certain music, certain rhythms and the inner music. Obviously you ask yourself now, 'What is this inner music? What is an inner rhythm?'

First it is important to put yourself in contact with this music. Without music there's no movement. It is certain that every particle is controlled by music. Everything we call solid matter is in fact composed of whirling atoms. Around these rotating atoms, electrons in their turn rotate. The atoms and electrons are, to put it in a simple way, bundles of energy that turn around a centre. All the things around us, the tables and chairs but also the walls, the whole of nature, are constantly in motion. These small particles move at an amazing speed. A speed so high that they give us the impression that everything around is solid.

You can compare it to electricity. When you enter a room and you switch on the light, you can see everything in the room. But in fact the electricity vibrates at a speed of fifty times per second. So every second, the light is switched on and off fifty times... Just like a movie which is made up of stills or fixed images which are projected so rapidly, one after another that we are not able to perceive the vibration and we experience a constant light. This is what we mean when we say that by the inner music everything whirls and dances.

Now let's take another step. The inner music is composed of two parts, like the two parts of a circle. The left half goes up while the right half goes down. Each rhythm creates a circle in space, a circle composed of two parts. The rhythm that is played in one half of the circle is opposed to the rhythm which is played in the other half of the circle. When the rhythm goes up we can describe it as *tan tanan*.

When the rhythm goes down it can be described as *tanan tan*. This is the principle of duality, comparable to the symbol of yin and yang. This symbol most of you know. This is the inner rhythm that makes everything in the universe turn. When you have listened carefully you have noticed that the ascending part of the rhythm is different from the descending part. The first rhythm is *tan tan tanan*, the second rhythm is *tanan tan*. One tan is missing out in the second part. So the circle is not closed and just this fact that the circle is not closed enables it to evolve. When the circle would be closed, every kind of development would be impossible and everything would, so to speak, 'turn around in circles'.

Therefore, the rhythm has the shape of a spiral, it ascends. This spiral, this up-going movement, provides the canal for the substantial evolution. The open part in the circle brings the energy up. This is a very important element in Sufism.

The experience of this spiralling movement gives you the opportunity to come closer to the sun, closer to the light. By playing the rhythms we polarise the energy in the cells of our body.

A Swiss researcher has come to the conclusion that certain vibrations of the Daf, the Persian frame-drum, can generate certain harmonious patterns in sand. This is exactly how the vibrations influence the cells in our body and especially in our heart. Because the energy is concentrated, the soul gets fed more. The soul, which is captured in our body, longs to rise, to fly and to move freely. By the playing of certain rhythms a passage is created giving the soul the possibility to leave the body and to experience the light. By polarising the energy, by playing the rhythms, the 'door of the heart' opens up and the soul can arise. It enables you to see the cells of your body from the outside. When we play a certain rhythm we are connected to others who play the same rhythm. The rhythms awake our heart, the hidden rhythms work on our soul. The rhythm becomes the instrument by which you can travel through the whole universe. It is like an elevator which takes you up."

Sheikh Kamel notices that many of his students are perplexed, so he continues to explain more about this subject.

"You should notice that you don't leave your body behind altogether. You go to other dimensions while in the same time you are here. In other dimensions you have the possibility to have other experiences. When the cells of your body are not polarised the soul cannot leave it. Rhythm is the way to polarise the cells in your body. When you repeat your Zekr, when you play Daf or when you are listening to the recitation, each time the electrons are re-directed and the heart becomes like a magnet.

A Sufi works exclusively on his heart. The heart is a gland that generates electricity. It has seven different points where this takes place. The seven layers of the heart are connected to the specific families of the rhythms. By polarising the energy in the heart it becomes a magnet. The functioning of the heart, of this magnet, creates a magnetic energy through the whole body. When the cells are polarised you are able to generate electricity around you. Then there is also the connection with other dimensions. It is magnetic energy.

The accumulation of this energy demands much work, it is a journey that goes a long way and it goes step by step. The rhythm cleanses us of the negative states; it is like a shower washing you clean. Meditation provides the substance that makes us radiate, while the Zekr makes our heart the vehicle of God's names. There must be a balance between the Zekr, the meditation and Daf playing. Inner balance is the most important for a student. It is not established in the head, but in the heart and it is the development in us of the substantial energy. Its emission is too subtle to be measured and therefore science is doubtful of it. The energy however can be experienced by others. The Sufis consider the heart as the door to other worlds, to other dimensions. The development of the substantial essence takes place outside the three dimensions of the universe we live in and the universe as we know it.

Before I told you that there are three ways to come in contact with the other dimensions; by meditation, by dreams and after death. The contact we make during the dream and after death however cannot be directed, but during the meditation it is possible, under the guidance of the teacher, to go in a certain direction.

Sometimes you feel sadness or have a feeling of nostalgia without knowing why. It is the soul that is captured in the body. When we hear a certain rhythm, the soul remembers its origin and the fact that it is captured in a body. In the beginning when we have started the exercise it can lead to a certain kind of sadness. Long ago the rhythms have invited the soul to come into the body and they are also able to free the soul from the body again. The heart is our origin and before the brain is created within the foetus, first the heart takes shape. After three weeks the divine order Kon ('Be', or 'To be')[5], comes and the heart starts beating, it is the joining of the heartbeat of the mother and the heartbeat of the foetus that invites the soul to come into the body. The same method, the invitation of the soul, we apply by playing Daf.

The mystics consider the middle part of the Daf to have the same vibration as the heart. As in mystical numerology seventy-two is the numerical representation of 'Kon', ('Be'), and the Daf can be divided into five, seventy-two degree segments which represent the five hidden inner senses, and give shape to the circular form of Daf (5x 72 = 360 degrees). Thus it is said that a person who holds the Daf holds his own heart, and all hearts are connected in the central part of the Daf.

Sufism is the science of the rhythms and letters of the alphabet. Even when you are not able to understand the meaning of a poem, you can understand it because its essence is love.

---

[5] The divine order 'Be' is considered the command for the act of creation itself. So as far as the foetus is considered is the moment when the soul enters the body of the foetus, after formation of its heart.

The rhythms provide a spiral staircase which goes up and which takes from the three dimensional and material world to the parallel world. Sufism is going step by step on this staircase by using the knowledge of the rhythms. In the mystical music notes are not being used, but the masters frame the letters with the mystical poetry. By doing so, the poems become the carrier of the inner rhythms and the inner poetry. The poems of Hafez, Rumi, Saadi and other mystical poets for instance are written within the frame of certain rhythms. The inner vibration indicates how a poem has to be written. It is a mathematical way of composing.

The poems are composed by certain laws and in the same time they provide a great freedom. The small territory of rationality is surrounded by a much larger world of synchronicity. The Sufi Master knows the secret of these rhythms. When recited, the poem's energy which lies condensed in it is again revived and works in our heart.

The poems have the colour; the signature of the poet and you can clearly distinguish the poems of Saadi, Hafez and Rumi because every poet is unique. Just like everyone is able to sing countless songs with his own distinct voice.

The Sufi Master knows the secret of the letters. The letters and the combination of letters have hermeneutical meanings. The secrets are embedded in the words. It is not a symbolic language because a symbol points to something else while in the hermeneutical language, the sentences, words and letters themselves are the carriers of the secrets. The essence is within them.

The Sufi alphabet exists between the rhythms and the meaning of the words. In ordinary language words usually have a single meaning; in Sufi language different meanings can be distinguished.

These meaning cannot be understood by someone who is not on this path. To put it in other words, a student understands the language in a direct way according to his level of development.

Long ago the Sufis chose the Farsi language to express themselves. The letters are ordered in four columns and here we recognise the four elements that form the material world: earth, water, fire and air. There are in total twenty-eight letters which means there are seven letters in each column. Each word in this language has a chemical and astrological meaning. For a Sufi the words have multiple meanings. The rhythms in the language work the same way as the language of the birds (that is hermetically). In this way a Sufi is able to communicate with the whole of existence. At home I play a rhythm and faraway you receive this rhythm. The rhythms are the carriers of the messages. The words also have their own numerical value.

The Alef, the letter A of the Persian alphabet, is straight like a cypress tree. It is independent and expresses the drive to strive upwards, to God. The Persian alphabet can be divided in letters which can be attached to Alef, and letters that cannot be attached to Alef. The Persian letter B for instance is a letter which can be attached to Alef.

Sheikh Kamel asks one of his students to write the letters on a big white paper in front of the group.

"When B is attached to Alef it becomes very small, it loses its big tail. The big tail is like the tail of a snake or a dragon. When B wants to submit to the Alef it has to lose its ego part. To experience the unity with the Alef, B has to sacrifice its independence and it has to become small and humble. So you have the choice to remain independent or to experience unity. But when you want to experience unity, you have to abandon the ego, the biggest part of yourself.

There are also letters like for instance the Persian H that has a round shape. When you attach yourself to this letter you wander around endlessly. Another example is the Persian letter M which has a movement that goes downwards.

So it is very important to decide to which letter you want to be connected. This is the Sufi alphabet; the message is transferred orally, from heart to heart.

The mystical poetry is recited; the reciting is called *Qawwali*. This reciting has nothing to do with the art of singing, one only progresses in this art of reciting when one becomes more advanced on the Path of the Substantial Evolution. The art of reciting is framed within the mystical rhythms. The transitions of the different letters and words are like black holes. Imagine that the energy flows in a certain direction, along with the words. When a certain letter has a, so to speak, reflecting character, the stream of energy goes backwards and runs into the energy which comes behind it. In this way a whirl of energy emerges.

When a spiral is created in a liquid substance it spirals downwards, think of a whirlpool for example, but when the whirling takes place in the air, in the form of gas; the spiral goes upwards. At these places in the poem energy is being added. Then there is acceleration to another level. These transitions are placed in certain quantities and at certain places in a poem. During the recitation the energy starts to whirl. This is the art of recitation, the music and the musical instruments have no influence on this process.

The mystical music consists of rhythm, harmony, melody and inner vibration. Recitation is the art to create and to direct the inner vibration. The function of the recitation can be compared to what was told before about the polarising of energy. In our normal state, the energy of our astral body is scattered through our whole physical body. During the recitation the energy is focused and is able to rise from the physical body.

A by-product of this rising of energy can be that your body makes uncontrolled movements. Some Iranian people are more sensitive to this effect than people from other countries. These effects however, are normal physical laws that are functioning in a natural way.

A lot of energy is needed to rise from the body, but once the energy is free from the body it takes less energy to stay in this state. It is only the recitation that produces this effect; it has nothing to do with the meaning of the words. The recitation produces the same energy in the hearts of all who are present. The whirling of this movement in the group can have an amplifying effect.

To return to the question of language, when the mystical poet speaks about wine, this is not a symbolic indication, but a description of the essence, the unknown essence of the wine. In the hermeneutical language the essence itself is present. Words can have different meanings; in some cases the same word even can have opposite meanings depending to the context; once again this emphasises the need for a teacher, a person who knows the language.

A mystic uses a word or sentence on many different levels. In a circle of friends one student can take a word totally differently compared to another friend, depending on his spiritual development. In this way we can describe the hermeneutical language as well; the comprehension of it by each individual depends on his substantial development. Rumi once said that he sometimes used the word 'no' when he meant 'yes'. You have to go deep within yourself to understand the substantial layers.

In fact it is only possible to understand spiritual poets like Saadi, Rumi and Hafez when you have reached the same depths as they have. It is the same for the language of the alchemists. Their language and the language of the mystics can be compared to the Koans of the Zen masters. So it seems almost impossible to understand the poems completely. Rumi said; "You can understand me when you turn your ears to eyes." Rumi knew the rhythms of the poetry and he used them. In order to understand Rumi better, we have to practice the rhythms.

Like the animals, we are physically fed by food, but the substance of a human being is fed by poetry. To listen to it is to experience it, but it is even more important to understand what you experience. Substantial knowledge is as light; therefore the soul can understand it."

Sheikh Kamel pauses to take some tea from the small glass next to him.

"The poetry works in three different ways: First there is the meaning of the words which influences the neocortex in our brain. Secondly, there is a musical influence which penetrates into a much older part of the brain, the paleocortex. This is the same for animals as for human beings. Thirdly, there is the mystical influence. The inner music influences all matters, all molecules and our soul. By the inner music all the molecules are stirred. It brings you in contact with the inner side of the universe.

There is a constant movement from reality to nothing, from darkness to light. We spoke about this before. This constant creation is a process we can hardly understand because it works at the speed of light.

Rumi said:

"You change from nothingness to existence

You can do anything you want

Sometimes you are sober, sometimes you are drunk

You can do anything you want."

We are able to perceive the light because we are on this side of existence. When we would have existed in darkness we would only have been able to understand the dark matter. Now, we only can experience darkness as the absence of light.

A seeker must not stop or hold on to the stage in which he is, but he constantly has to move on. It is even important to deny the state which you are in. To grow is the essence of evolution and to deny the state which you are in is a positive attitude regarded in the light of continuous evolution. Of course, the soul will experience a certainty which has to be denied in turn to grow to the next stage. The real security for the soul is to trust and to know that there will be a new certainty. The cage of a parrot can be beautiful, but it remains a cage. A seeker has to travel to other dimensions and when he has witnessed them this material world will appear very small and tight for him. Heart and soul may be small in appearance, but as the development of nanotechnology is discovering, in a small particle everything is hidden. The same is true for our heart and soul.

To say something more on the rhythms: The Sufi Masters distinguish twenty-four families of rhythms. Every family looks like a pyramid, a pyramid of thirty stairs. The student starts at the first step in order to climb step by step to the top of the first pyramid. Then he starts climbing the next pyramid and so on. At last he arrives at the peak of perfection, in the house of the Simorg. It is a total of seven hundred and twenty steps and thus he discovers the secret of creation. The number seven hundred twenty corresponds to the word Kon which means be.

God spoke this word and the universe was created. The universe is the crystallisation of the names of God.

When you cut an apple in half you see a circle divided in five equal segments, each part corresponds with seventy-two degrees. Five multiplied by seventy-two makes three hundred sixty degrees. This is a natural division.

On the Daf, the Persian frame drum we play, we see the same division. We can only play on two segments; the other three await the vibration in silence. The Daf is the symbol of an advanced Sufi. Its round shape is the sign of perfection and the Sufis gather in a circle. The skin is the skin of the master under which the student is protected. The rings are a sign of acceptance and obedience. When the Daf is in silence, this symbolises patience."

Sheikh Kamel pauses while everyone remains silent.

"For a Daf it is not good to be silent for a long time, so take your Daf."

Chapter 4: Time and events

When Sheikh Kamel has taken his seat in front of his students he shows them a CD.

"Look" he says, "A CD contains a great deal of information on a small disc. This is a CD filled with music. It can be regarded as a compilation of time. When you play the CD you put the time in motion; the time flows from the future to the past. When we look at the straight form of Alef, we can see the shape of an hourglass in it, with the time streaming downward. The Persian letter H, which has a round shape, you can regard as a compilation of time. When the CD I hold in my hand contains no music, it is empty, without time. I have the disc in my hand and thus I am holding the time between my fingers.

Whatever you see during the day, whatever you look at, always you look at the past. The light, by which you can see everything around you, needs a very small fraction of a second to reach your eyes. So information needs time to come from you to me.

In case of the future it works differently, because the future is created by you from the present. When we develop ourselves on the Path of the Substantial Evolution, we start to long for the future. This is one of the secrets of the path.

Everybody is constantly exposed to the past. Even when I expect something, I expect something from the past."

Some of the students are very surprised by this remark. They look at Sheikh Kamel who decides to explain more about the subject.

"Imagine that I expect two guests and I go to the station to meet them. And imagine that each one of them will arrive by a different train and that they will arrive at the same time, let's say four o'clock, at the station. I go to the station and yes, shortly after each other, both trains arrive and I am reunited with my friends. The train of one of my friends however, has departed at one o'clock in the afternoon while the other friend had to catch the train at ten o'clock in the morning. So, both of my friends departed in the past to meet me in the present.

The present, the moment of 'now', is in our heart!

At the edge of the CD time starts and it ends in the middle. If I play the CD the music will go on for let's say one hour. This one hour can be called personal time of the CD. From the present we create the future. Imagine that you have thirty CDs and one hour of time, in this one hour you are only able to listen to one CD. At home, I have a television and I can receive hundred channels. However, I can only look at one channel at a time. Each of the hundred channels are on air twenty-four hours a day and continuously they broadcast their programmes. So time is a mysterious and paradoxical phenomenon. We live day by day, but we are hardly aware of the expiring of time. Your personal time is expiring continuously and all is meeting in the here and now. The awareness of time is hidden from us, and our personal time is limited, it ends at a certain moment.

When I look at a television programme I think I gain something, but in the same time I lose the other ninety-nine programmes.

Often I decide for myself that I am the one who makes the right choice for me. But in the same time, there are people that know the content of thirty CDs. It is better to consult them.

When you create something, you win time. You materialise the future; you make it concrete by your actions. But even when you are creating continuously, it will be impossible to know the future.

Sometimes you decide to go and do something and it does not work out, no matter how hard you try, it is not within God's plans. When we live in the world we have to be active and in the same time we have to be full of trust. Even when you do not reach a certain goal in your life or even if you fail, you don't need to worry. There is a hidden meaning which maybe you will understand later. When time passes by maybe you will see the reason for the failure of a certain enterprise.

When something does not work out the way we want it we can be happy because it goes the way God wants it to go. This way of looking at events is very hard for our ego. Our ego does not accept this approach and it wants to control the situation and have everyone within its power.

God lets you try in your own way and in the future you will see the results. When you begin to realise that God loves you, you will get a totally different taste of life.

You can compare yourself with a seeker in a boat on the wide ocean. It is better to row along with the stream and the wind. Hafez, a Sufi poet, said: "We are sailors and from the ship we look at your friendly face. We set sail towards the Beloved."

Columbus was a very famous traveller, who did everything to arrange his plans in the best possible way. At the same time there were a lot of people praying for him. This is the visible and the invisible aspect. You cannot know where the stream is leading you. For example a serious illness can be a clue telling you that you are going in a wrong way.

It is about my own decisions, for these decisions I am responsible. Often people dare not to decide for themselves and then they hide this fact saying that everything is God's will. You can state that is was God's will that the African and the Asian continent were connected to each other. There were people who were planning to dig a canal from the Mediterranean Sea to the Indian Ocean. With the help of God this canal was realised. It is like the melting of two paths. When you leave all the initiative to God or with other people you allow them to shape your life. It is, again I say this, about the decisions I take within my own reach. I am not responsible for the weather or for the social circumstances of a whole nation. On one hand I can try to emigrate to the U.S.A. and on the other hand, the government of France can force me to leave the country. This indicates the difference. When we ask something deeply sincere then God will provide for us, often in a way we don't expect. With our reasoning often we are not able to find a solution. It is better to be poor and empty. This makes it easier for a spiritual solution to appear.

Again and again there is this inner question: 'Can I accept the will of God?'

One of the students asks: "When I am enthusiastic to do something, is this a sign that I am going in the right direction?"

"That cannot be said with certainty" Sheikh Kamel answers, "Enthusiasm can easily be a product of my ego. It is necessary to purify your actions and your thoughts again and again in order to flow more and more together with God. Within this world, not only the law of causality functions, also non-causal laws like the law of series, the law of probability, the law of synchronicity are functioning.

All events in the world happen in cycles. A cycle can be compared to someone who is in the middle of the sea in a storm. He has to wait until the storm is over, he has no alternative. Events take place in cycles; a cycle can be described as a series of events happening after another. Cycles are inevitable, they occur, you have to deal with them and they always end.

When one cycle ends, another one starts.

Our task is not to identify ourselves with the circumstances that a cycle may bring, but to be oriented towards God. By remaining in the cycles in this way we have the opportunity to increase the capacities of our soul.

When Joseph was in Egypt he had a dream in which he saw seven fat and seven thin cows. These cows symbolise the cycles. The cycles cannot be changed, but we can prepare ourselves. It is a constant exercise to be near to God in the midst of the cycles.

Saadi says: "Drop money in the river Euphrates and God will provide a solution for your problem in the middle of the desert." This indicates the non-causal way in which things are connected.

Often the poems of Hafez are consulted for non-causal problems. Usually we try to solve a problem with our mind and when this does not succeed we consult someone. Hafez was an empty canal to the unseen world. Someone who is authorised can give you advice. The one who gives you advice will explain your situation to you, but he will not give you a solution for your problem.

So when we are facing a problem or a certain situation we have to be stable in front of it.

Secondly, we can ask the advice of someone who is authorised to give advice. And thirdly, we can prepare ourselves during the times everything goes well for times when we have to face problems.

Once there was a merchant who had lost all his money and in the end he went to a mystic to ask his advice. "Take the money which lies under the doormat" the mystic said and the merchant did so. "When you have solved your problems please return the money to me" he added. The merchant went relieved and within a short time his business prospered again. Time went by, but he forgot to return the money. Years later again he ran out of money and totally at a loss he remembered the mystic. Once again he visited him and asked for help. He told his problem and the mystic told: "Take the money that lies under the doormat". When the merchant reached for the money, the place was empty. Surprised he asked the mystic why there was no money. The mystic answered: "Because you forgot to bring it back the first time you took it."

During good times we can do good actions in order to have a reserve for harder times. You have to consider however that the goal is not to store a lot of positive actions, but that it is more important that you dedicate everything you do to God.

Time and events

When you are facing a problem, be patient. The biggest problem you can have is the problem of love. Patience is easy when times are hard, but to be patient is very difficult when you are in love. The most difficult test God can give to someone is to let him fall in love. Love and patience are like fire and water, it is impossible to bring them together in one place. For the problem of love there is no solution. Love is beyond the causal and the non-causal laws.

When you are in love, you are like a garden, a garden longing for the spring. When you are in love, you are like a candle, standing solid while burning with longing. You burn and you melt by longing. The candle becomes smaller and smaller. The candle is not afraid of the fire in its top and at the same time it is standing in the water. He is the lover who is between the water and the fire. He is the symbol of longing and patience. Within another context, the candle can be the symbol of the beloved; the lover is represented as a butterfly, the butterfly that wants to melt in the fire. Together they melt into unity. The lover is waiting his whole life for this moment of unity. The lover lives in darkness and waits for the morning. He is the garden waiting for the first breeze of spring, the flower waiting for the first morning light.

In the garden lives the nightingale. The nightingale waits as long as three hundred sixty days for the flower to unfold its petals. She has to wait a whole year for five days in the company of the flower. A year has twelve periods of thirty days; five days don't count as normal days in the mystical calendar. The whole year the nightingale is waiting between the bushes and thorns. The thorns are always there while the flower only blooms for five days. The path of the mystic is difficult because it is always surrounded by thorns. The five days left over are a period of transition; they are looked on as a bridge. During these days the door to heaven is open.

The nightingale waits for the flowering, the flower is a book and its petals are the leaves from which the nightingale reads the secrets. The nightingale just reads us a few pages because she knows that we cannot understand too much at once. The flower itself is not at all interested in the nightingale; it wants to go to heaven as quickly as possible.

Wintertime is cold and it lasts a long time. My nostalgia will never leave me. The path is very difficult, yet in the same time it is very sweet. Lover and beloved meet each other on the bridge. In the calendar of love you have to be very patient. Even for a great mystic like Hafez this was often very difficult. As a lover, Hafez is totally open with his beloved and so he also writes about his difficulties to his beloved in some of his poems. He asks the King of Destination to change the path. The goal is good, but he finds it hard to accept that the butterfly has to burn in the flame and that the flower only blooms five days for the nightingale. Hafez would like to suffer less before being united with the beloved. But this is how it is.

Hafez says: "Within the circle of destination we are the point of surrender."

We are like a point on a circle without any will of our own, like the pin of a compass always pointing to the north without any individual will. The circle of the compass is like the rotation of the sun, the sun that is travelling in the sky. In the summer the sun is strong and gives much warmth and in winter the sun is pale, radiating no warmth. It is always turning without a will of its own.

In the circle of destination we are the wandering point in the compass of the universe. There is someone who lets the sun turn.

Rumi travelled from Afghanistan, Shams[6] travelled from Tabriz in the north of Iran to Konya in Turkey. At some point they met. Later Rumi begged Shams to stay with him, but this was impossible for Shams. So they parted ways. Sometimes the sun is within a good house, sometimes the sun is within a bad house, and this is something we have to accept."

---

[6] Shams Tabrizi was Rumi's inspirational master.

Chapter 5: The relation with the Master

Rumi said to his Master: "You are the crystallised heart."

Once there was a Master who gave to each one of his students a seed and asked them to grow this seed. Of course all did their best. After some weeks the students gathered again and everyone had a pot with a young plant in, except for one student. It seemed the seed of this student had not sprouted. The Master looked at all the little plants, but he only praised the student who had not grown a young plant. He was the only one who had exactly followed the instructions of the Master. Before the Master distributed the seeds, he had cooked them all.

Attentively Sheikh Kamel looks at his students. As was to be expected, he has taken his seat in front of the group.

"Today I want to speak with you about the relation between the Master and the student. It is an important subject especially now that human relations have changed dramatically during the past decades. In the past, the teacher – also the teacher at the regular schools – had a natural authority.

Figure 3- Depiction of the Master (the Swan) and her disciples (cygnets)

The students respected this authority which, in most cases, was right. However, in present times a teacher is a person who might know more of his specific field of knowledge, but who is, concerning all other aspects, as ordinary as everybody else.

When travelling the spiritual path, we ourselves are the subject of our study and exercises and usually we are only very dimly aware of our inner state. When we decide to attend this school we have to realise that we are not here just for acquiring mental knowledge, neither simply to learn certain practises. A central pillar in Sufism is the relation with the teacher and, contrary to ordinary life, this relation does not stop outside the classroom, but it gradually pervades more and more into the life of the student. Today we will speak about this.

Every spiritual school has a discipline. Without discipline you will not achieve results. A path without discipline is not a serious path. Holding on to a discipline only depends on your ego. Discipline is very hard for the ego. A good teacher looks very harsh because he chooses against your ego.

We always have, within ourselves, ways to deal with two personalities, our true self and our false self. This false personality we call 'the ego'. Its manifestation, outwardly in certain ways of behaviour, but also inwardly, like in certain thoughts, is called the *nafs* by the Sufis. A Sufi tries to gain control over his false personality. In other words, he tries to control his *nafs*. He tries to develop his essential, his substantial self. Our ego is for a large part determined by our unconscious behaviour, our upbringing and our reflection on our social activities.

When still young, a child starts to think and reflect on his own behaviour and to adjust his behaviour to others and his environment. In general, these reflections are deformed and because of this, egoistic behaviour starts to grow. So the person becomes oriented on the maintenance and expansion of the false self. Of course, this is only a superficial indication of the ego. Thousands of scholars and therapists are continuously working to understand the human behaviour. Sufism, however, is concerned with our essential self.

This essential part of our self we call the substantial aspect. This substantial aspect is what we learn to discover and develop on this path. The development of the substantial aspect is difficult especially because the Sufi is not allowed to show his essential being. This may seem strange, but it is not, when you realise that the ego likes to boast, likes to talk and likes to feel special. So the ego is not satisfied. It is for this reason that this path is being called 'the path of poverty'.

In these times it is very difficult to develop your substantial reality. The world is full of illusions which continuously distract us when we want to focus on one goal.

When we stay at the surface we might think we have all the options at our fingertips and we can choose what and when we want, but in fact we wander from illusion to illusion without penetrating into the depths. A lot of movements and individual persons compete to get our attention. They try to persuade us by playing on the weak points of our ego and, for instance, to suggest that the spiritual path is effortless, and that it is very easy to accomplish.

In present times, especially in the West, individuality, and in particular independence, is emphasised, and authority is something which is criticised or at least considered suspect. 'Everybody is equal' is a much-heard slogan which only leads to the fact that people listen shortly and superficially and judge quickly. The activities of false gurus and dangerous sects get a lot of media attention. So, most of the people are very reserved towards spiritual paths that ask a deep connection and strong determination of their students. Another difficulty is the false expectation of a lot of people who think that on the spiritual path the student only has to receive what is being given.

The reality, however, is that you have to give and not take on this path. You have to be here for others and for God and not in the first place for yourself. The more you give, the more you receive; the more water you let flow, the more pours in. This is a logical and apparently obvious fact, but it is very hard to apply. One of the glasses the ego likes to wear is to look in every situation for its own benefit and how to take advantage of it.

When you ponder about this for a while you have to conclude that these glasses are very often on your nose and that it is more the rule than the exception that you want your own profit to come first.

When we act positively the results are positive, when we act negatively the results are negative and this is something we cannot accept. Instead of accepting it, we try to find all kinds of rationalisations and excuses to put the responsibility somewhere else; we blame the situation, other people or even our own habits.

In Sufism we have to learn to accept that everything which is good comes from God. So always be attentive to the goodness of God and not to your own actions. This is very hard and so it is good to think about this long and deeply. Often the student is unsure about his progress on the path. A good way to measure this is to verify to what extent you control your lust, your aggression, your greed, and your jealousy.

A Sufi thinks about his deeds at the end of the day and is determined to do it better the next day. A very practical example of this is not to expect a reward for a positive action. It is the goodness of God that counts and not my actions. A human being that is not following a spiritual discipline is constantly under the domination of his ego, while a Sufi is under the eye of God.

When two Sufis argue, they respect each other's point of view and they often prefer the meaning of the other to their own meaning.

A Sufi like Shah Nematollah Vali is always in search for the pearl of the substantial self and nothing else. Shah Nematollah Vali travelled greatly during his life. One time he unfolded a beautiful tent which he had received as a present. Another Dervish was wondering 'Why does he have such a beautiful tent?' Then Shah Nematollah Vali left his tent and the Dervish followed him. In a nearby village, Shah Nematollah Vali entered a house and at that moment the Dervish asked permission to go back because he had forgotten his pipe. Shah Nematollah Vali told him that he was attached to his pipe. Egos attach to power, money and also to a pipe. Shah Nematollah Vali was not attached to his beautiful tent.

Jesus is also an important example for the Sufis. Jesus was always poor. It is very difficult to be very powerful and at the same time poor. When we want to control our ego it is better to start today than tomorrow and it is better to prefer the meaning of others to our own meaning.

What about your own mistakes? Are you able to see your own mistakes? Can you look at every action of yourself objectively and decide to act better the next time?

When I am satisfied with my behaviour I am never motivated to improve myself.

Hafez says; "Even when it is not your mistake, it is better to admit that it is your mistake." Now this is very hard and it takes much practice to reach this state. This is the foundation of tolerance. We need to be more tolerant."

Sheikh Kamel looks around, what he has said seems to be clear and there are no questions.

"It is the same with criticism. Never criticise anybody else, only yourself. Often with the best intentions, but based on our own judgmental perspective, we start to advise others because we think we know better; it is then we immediately forget ourselves and we put ourselves, without knowing, in the role of a judgemental advisor.

Rumi lived in the same time as the great destructor Genghis Khan. Still he never criticised him, because, as he said "He is like a mirror for us. We ourselves also are a Genghis Khan. If we would have the power of Genghis Khan we would also be as destructive as he is."

So respect, or even prefer, the opinion of somebody else to your own opinion.

Of course 'to respect' does not mean that we should approve everything. When somebody acts badly in our opinion we certainly can be critical, but we must judge only the action, not the person.

Destruction is never good, but we must not judge Genghis Khan, only his actions. In the end we are very well able to do the same as he. It is important to be aware of good and bad actions and to choose the positive actions.

For a Sufi it is important to see God in everything. The heart is small, it has only place for one Beloved. You cannot love the world and God in the same moment; you have to make a choice. God is present in all aspects of life. Try to see God in everything; it will completely change your life.

When I want to walk the Sufi path my ego is very well able to mislead me. I can for instance decide to postpone a certain decision in order to decide better. The answer to this is that a Sufi student cannot decide by himself. He has to have a teacher who instructs him. For my ego this is very difficult, but when I am my own teacher, then I am taught by my ego. A student is not able to travel to God by himself. So, a good teacher is not someone who satisfies you, on the contrary, he has to criticise you. He must not feed your ego. It is hard to be criticised, you would rather receive compliments to be satisfied.

Hafez said: "Put wine on your praying rug when the teacher asks you to do so."

In other words, follow the instruction of your teacher instead of your own ideas, even when the instruction is opposite to your own point of view. As you are, you are only very dimly aware of your

The relation with the Master

nafs, the bad habits of your ego. The teacher knows and sees this. This exactly is the difference between the student and the teacher.

We need a teacher who is connected to God because when we don't have a teacher, the ego is our teacher. And the ego is the worst teacher. Shams did not want to be the teacher of Rumi, it was Rumi who wanted to be the student of Shams when he recognised and discovered the truth of Shams. Shams only wanted to be connected to God without having students. When Rumi discovered the truth he concluded that the universe was empty without Shams.

For a seeker it is very important to find somebody who is more ahead on the path than he is. He has to ask God for help in this situation. Only afterwards Rumi realised that he had to become empty in order to be filled with the lessons of Shams. Rumi was an important professor and Shams did not want to be the teacher of an important professor. In the end, Shams agreed to teach him, but after some time he left Rumi again.

When you want to study music or you want to become a doctor, immediately you agree that you need a good teacher, but in case of ourselves we hesitate and object. Exams are necessary, also for a good student. The moment you don't get any more exams, God has let you go. It is not about being a good Sufi; it is about becoming a good Sufi! The road to God is endless because God is infinite. Constantly we have to go on and accept that we must to go on. When you stop you are no longer a Sufi. Some think that when they are on the path they will receive privileges or special rights or they think that the path will be easier.

Hafez says: "Love is easy in the beginning, and then the difficulties arise."

The master is the master and nothing else. He has to be able to teach the lessons and not just by words alone. What he teaches he must have accomplished himself. There are a lot of people who want to be on the spiritual path, but there are few teachers.

The contact with the teacher starts as a revolution in your heart, you are attracted by a strong feeling that you cannot deny. The lover does not want to go in this direction and sometimes he is very scared, but an invisible rope draws him to the beloved.

Gradually, the student will discover more and more the value of the master. This produces a love and this love becomes stronger and stronger. A great example of this love in Sufism is the love of Rumi for Shams. Rumi was as the sugar that dissolved in the ocean of Shams. After this he crystallised. In the immense love, the attachment to the Master, we lose our animal needs and we become a spiritual being.

The love to the Master changes the hormones in the paleocortex of the brain and so the animal functions get weakened and eventually they stop. In the beginning Rumi was ecstatic with joy when Shams was near to him, afterwards it became sadness and this changed his spiritual state. By his love and his connection to Shams he changed. Shams is an alchemist, he is able to change the spiritual state of somebody. When Shams had left, Rumi became a musician and he concentrated on playing the rhythms on the Daf. He transmitted the same vibrations that were created by Shams. This was the inner music of his Master. He attracted many students.

When a student wanted to be educated in the Tekyeh of Rumi in Konya, first he had to serve the community for a 1,000 days. Once we visited the Tekyeh of Rumi in Konya which has now become a museum where there are many artefacts from former days. There is a picture in the Tekyeh representing a barber with two swords. Every new day is full of imagination and time after time the student has to offer his head in order that the wishes of his ego are cut. The disciple does not have to worry. Shah Nematollah Vali says: "Don't worry my friend because I care for you. I am your only friend in the visible and invisible world."

The student must have a special psychological condition. The Master feels if the student has this condition and if the student is willing to work with it. Still the Master will not ask you or force you, the conditions you have to create by yourself.

A Sufi is a person who lives in the society and who has a family, a job and social responsibilities; but at the same time focuses on being empty. This is very difficult. The beginning of the relation between the student and the Master is a dream with a spiritual message. The Master gives us instructions in accordance to our own capacity; this is necessary to keep the balance. By the Zekr and the rhythms, the inner substance of the student changes. So, the divine energy leads you to the Master. The Master is like an ocean, but he presents himself like a cup of water.

When the student grows he discovers more and more of the reality of the Master. The advice of the Master is more important than your own ideas; still the Master will not provide you the solutions. He teaches you a method by which you can search with your heart. Without developing this capacity by yourself, you will always need a Master and thus you will become dependent to him.

A real teacher teaches you how to be independent. Often people are very afraid or critical of the Master, they are afraid to lose themselves, even if their situation is very bad, or they expect the Master to be a magician, able to perform all kinds of miracles to solve their problems. When you are not a good student the Master will not criticise you, he leaves you to yourself. When you think you have to be your own teacher than your ego will be your teacher.

You make in full freedom your own decision to go to a teacher.

The teacher will ask a certain discipline of you. Discipline is, like determination and patience, and is very important on the path.

The material world passes by very quickly while the substantial development progresses very slowly. Discipline is the foundation of the relation between the student and the Master. Within this relation the one who aspires to travel this path takes the role of the student. Again this is very difficult for the ego. Only then he receives the teachings. When you work on yourself you receive new lessons and attention.

The teacher teaches, he doesn't just tell mere stories or fairy tales. Discipline is the rope by which we tie down the ego. It is important to have regular contact with the teacher. A common rule however cannot be given for this aspect. The frequency of the contact is subject to the laws of synchronicity and not to causal laws. At a certain stage it is enough to establish an invisible contact. The relation between the Master and the student is individual because every individual is different and everybody needs specific exercises which conform to his own capacities.

Some time ago I sent you by email an old picture of two birds, a big and a small one, exactly the same. They represent the Master and the student. The birds are exactly the same; one is only bigger than the other. When you are like a bird you are able to fly to another reality. The old bird is the teacher; he is timeless, so he is young again. The Master is like a father for you and gradually he grows into much more than a father. The Master is like a big eagle, under his wings many smaller birds and insects are able to fly to the top of the mountain. In the end the Master becomes the creator of your own being. You discover a black hole within yourself and you enter it. This is something which cannot be learned outwardly. The rhythms, the music and the calligraphy are in the end just an excuse to be in contact with each other.

The Master does not present himself as a Master; he is not in search of you. You are the one who decides. When you feel a deep longing, ask God to show you the right Master. Ahead of us is a big mountain, its top is in the clouds and its roots are deep in the earth. We seek the connection with the hidden reserve of water. In our life we can respond in three ways to a situation; in a rational way, in an emotional way and in a mystical way. When you try to understand a certain event in a mystical way you try to find out what the lesson of this event is. By doing so, you learn about yourself. Normally, in daily life, we try to dominate circumstances and people around us when we don't understand a certain aspect. I make a judgement about it and I judge the people around me. In this case, I consider myself as the other person and I start to explain how much better I would behave, if I was in his place. I judge by my ego. Mystical evaluation however urges me to investigate the mystery without judgements. Now I have an instrument by which I can investigate myself. In this way I can see to what extent my ego is active.

Once, a seeker had travelled a long way, in order to find a Master. After many recommendations, eventually he knocked at the door of the house of a famous Master. The wife of the Master opened the door and started to speak elaborately about all the shortcomings of her husband. In the end the seeker left the house disappointed. On the road he met the master, who had held a snake like a stick and was accompanied by a tamed lion. This master had gained control over both.

In daily life people act and deal with each other from their ego. The Master is different. That is why you have to become either the student of the Master or the friend of the Master. You cannot be the friend and the student of the Master at the same time. In all circumstances you experience you have to find out for yourself what the lesson in these events is for you. When the student forgets his place he starts judging situations rationally or emotionally. From time to time the student passes exams; to measure to what extent the ego is active. Joseph for example received an important exam when he suffered from the consequences of his brothers' jealousy. Sometimes the seekers are put in the oven of an exam. The difficulties were caused by jealousy and this is terrible, even worse than a snake bite. These exams are necessary because it is only by attraction and friction that water starts to move. The grinding stone that grinds the seeds turns because of the power of the water, but the water itself is invisible.

The attraction between the student and the Master is there in order to continue this process so the stone keeps turning. When the attraction is gone the Master is unable to be in contact with the student. This contact is only possible thanks to circumstances in which the ego is 'sleeping'. When the ego 'wakes' the stream stops. So you have to be very alert. As long as you wander on the ocean it doesn't matter, but when you start to move into one direction, more resistance is evoked.

The relation with a Master can be compared to an acrobat in the circus. On the high wire he shows his art, but he has to rely on the one on the ground, the one who catches him. The catcher needs to be very alert; one moment of sleepiness can be fatal.

When you are cut from the image of your Master immediately you are in a risky situation.

There is the possibility that you are seduced by the Antichrist. The way of the Antichrist to lure you away is by building a wall between you and your Master. It is even more dangerous when the Antichrist presents himself as a friend, someone you trust. There are a lot of people with the intention to capture others who want to set out on a spiritual path. This is very dangerous when you have so much trust in the one who leads you astray. When you have chosen a Master it is important that you have total trust in him. You will need this trust on the spiritual path and when this trust is abused it is likely that you will never trust again. The development of your mind stops and you will not grow further.

Seekers constantly pose themselves questions about these bad experiences and are not able to digest it. Therefore never ask for the reason of a certain exam or test, for instance a serious illness or the death of another. You only need to be totally trustful because you can never fully understand the reason and significance of a certain event. Someone who has little trust is very vulnerable to bad circumstances. When you remain confident after a bad experience your trust will grow and you will become stronger. When you lose your trust your soul dies.

When a weightlifter does not increase the weights he lifts he will not grow. He has to lift heavier and heavier things in order to develop. It is also possible that you want to be more and more independent of the others. The first sign you need to be aware of in this case is that others appear to be far away from you. Also you can become excited or restless. In this moment you need to realise that something is going on in you and you should start immediately to clean yourself.

Inwardly the chemical composition is changed and thus your reactions and behaviour become different. You only notice the last part; that your behaviour has become different. When you become aware of this, you have to connect with the Master as quickly as possible. Apart from this, you need to examine carefully what preceded this feeling. Check every situation and event that happened before this feeling appeared. By doing this you are able to wash the stains. It is a long process, but when you wait it only will take longer to clean yourself again.

Be critical and analytical in a mystical way. When you dig deeper and deeper within yourself, your ego dies. The stream is always there and you receive more and more from the Master.

The relation between the Master and the student is a lifelong relation. The Master always holds one end of the cord, it is up to the student to hold on or to let go."

> *Long ago a young traveller came to the bank of a huge river. A powerful stream separated the people living in a little village called 'Slumber' from the other side of the river where they had their jobs. Near the stream lived an old man with an old boat. He was the ferryman and his task was to ferry the people of this sleepy village across the river. In the morning he*

The relation with the Master

took them to the other side and in the evening he collected them again. The daily journey had become a routine for the villagers. The young man saw that the boat was old and that the ferryman was repairing it constantly while nobody paid any attention. The young traveller decided to stay for a while with the old man.

On a certain day the ferryman spoke: "I see a huge stream of water developing and coming our way and I see dark clouds and storms at the horizon. I will have to make a bigger and stronger boat and I need help for this. Nobody from the village responded to his question because everybody was busy and they said: 'We don't see any dark clouds at all and please consider our situation as well, while you are with your boat we have to work as well. Of course we come to you when we want to travel to the other side of the river'".

They did not care for the old man and his boat even though they relied on his ability to maintain his boat for ferrying them across the river. Not for a second did occur to them that the old man did this job just for them and not for himself. They did not realise that without him they would not be able to cross the river and that the old man could perfectly well take care of himself, that he did not need them. It did not occur to them that the ferryman could easily go to another place and offer his services there. The day came that the people came to the river without finding a trace of the ferryman or his boat. They could not find a solution as they stood there. Clouds filled the sky and a storm started.

Thirty years later, at another spot near the river there was a little town called 'Shadow'. Near the stream there lived a ferryman who took the people across the river. His attention was fully with his boat and the people did not care for him. He had the features of the young traveller who had departed long ago with his Master from the village 'Slumber'.

Chapter 6: Fanaticism

The gathering starts by listening to the sound of the flute. After a short silence, Sheikh Kamel starts to talk.

"Today I want to speak with you about dogmatism, blind belief and fanaticism. Often we take religious dogmas for the truth, dogmas that have not been investigated. Instead of an assumed religion, which has not been investigated, reasoning is a more reliable source of truth.

We started by listening to the flute, the flute which is hollow and therefore free of desires, superstition and fanaticism. Fanaticism can be described as a blind belief to an idea or a doctrine. It starts by taking something for granted, or by assuming the authority of somebody. A fanatic is an immature person lacking knowledge and honesty and following a hierarchical authority. Of course there can be numerous causes for this type of behaviour, but it would take too long to discuss them in this meeting.

Blind belief or blindly accepting and following certain ideas excludes the use of reasoning and logical thinking. Each individual should try to find the truth within himself, but sometimes, when you see the reality of your own truth, you can be considered to be a fanatic as well, because your own truth is a part of yourself. In this case, you ascribe the truth to your ego, and by doing so, you identify the truth with yourself. You are like a piece of cotton, drenched in water, the cotton and the water cannot be separated.

Fanaticism can be seen in many different forms. However, most deeply rooted form of fanaticism is found in religion. The word religion originates from the Latin words, 're' which means 'again', and 'ligare' which means 'to connect'. Together this points at the joining of a human being with a supreme creator: God. Religion without philosophy becomes fanaticism and philosophy without spirituality only leads to mental reflections.

Religion needs to have a clear, critical mind, transcendental knowledge and a heart, in other words, a transcendental orientation. By ascertaining the presence of these two elements – reason and the transcendental knowledge of the heart – we are able to distinguish religion and fanaticism.

For instance, when we think of the crusades, we learn that people in those days were convinced that they were working and fighting for God, so they could not perceive the human suffering that was the result of their actions. When we make this principle universal, we can conclude that followers of a certain tradition often regard people that follow another path as less worthy than themselves. In the worst case, they persecuted them. In both the Eastern and Western world, there are historical moments which have influenced the development of fanaticism with results that are evident today.

About a 1,000 years ago, the Islamic scholar Al-Ghazaly broke away from the theories and more critical methods used by philosophers before him like Plato and Aristotle. He believed that a human being does not need to think for himself, but that he only has to live according to the laws and words of the Prophets and Holy Scriptures. His reasoning was; 'when you think, you start to doubt and when you start to doubt you can no longer believe.' So the phrases attributed to the Saints became instructions and laws.

Texts had to be lived up to in detail and the reasoning behind them could not be clarified, let alone discussed. There are many prescriptions, for instance with which foot one has to enter a house, which arm has to be put into which sleeve first, what kind of colour of clothes one needs to wear on a certain day and so on. A result of these often very strict rules people began to question if they were living in the right way. Violation of the rules had consequences for the afterlife as a minimum, but often also in the life on earth. In this way, one ends up in a straitjacket, as the result of indoctrination.

This system was and is extended by adding all kinds of rules and sayings ascribed to a holy person or to a Saint. So, when somebody starts to comment or ask critical questions, immediately this is taken as criticism to the Saint. Because of this it becomes impossible to investigate the individual spiritual paths or other ways, such as Sufism. Often this is combined with a lack of interest and a lack of understanding which leads to a critical attitude towards the path that is followed.

A fanatic is convinced that he is the only one following the right faith and by doing so, heaven will be his reward while the others go to hell. To avoid this way of thinking, the first step can be made by questioning, by putting things in doubt. First try to understand the human being and afterwards what is said and not first what is said and only then the human being, "I love the truth more than my Master and the more truth my Master tells, the bigger my love for my Master."

Each question, every problem, every mystery, in short everything we encounter in our lives, has its own truth and this truth you have to search within yourself. Do not rely on what somebody else is telling you. It will not fit within your own truth, but only with the truth of the one who says it. So when someone says to you: "Just believe this and that because it is right, you don't have to ponder about it", be careful.

Descartes said: "I am, because I doubt everything."

What is reality? Reality is a concept. The difference between reality and truth is that reality 'happens', it takes place within the frame of space and time. Truth does not belong to the material world, but it is a science, it is the science of God. When you are able to discover that truth is the science of God then you are able to distinguish how the truth differs from the reality of the material world. The issue of self-censoring must not be underestimated. Because you have the tendency to believe and because this is much easier and less exhaustive you are not willing to listen, to investigate and to think.

When we know ourselves we realise that this is the reality of being one; we realise that we are a group of people with a spiritual connection. Rumi says in a poem: "In unity we are connected as seekers on the path of love. Unity transcends the truth and every kind of belief. This light bears no colour."

The fire of love will consume fanaticism and the way to fight fanaticism is to radiate love. With the Daf we fight fanaticism wherever it manifests. Our body is like a boat on the ocean of the heart and the waves that come from our heart make our body move. This cannot be understood, this is the place where thinking stops. This ecstasy is the first step on the path of love.

The second step is to be totally consumed by the fire. Our reason can put forth many questions, but for a lot of questions there is no solution. The function of thinking is to pose questions and not to find solutions.

Theologians put mankind in front of the uneasy 'if not, then...' choice. For a theologian like Al-Ghazaly every creature, every being in the universe had a numeral value, each one was accepted or rejected, you were a believer or a heretic. His world was a world of two separated and opposite camps; fanaticism will not allow a peaceful coexistence of several ways of living.

From a psychological point of view, fanaticism is connected with the idea of fear or hate. Exactly these ideas and emotions take a central place within the mind of a fanatic. They prevent him from realising the connection to his soul. The intolerant fanatic resorts to violence.

The fanatic bans people, imprisons them and executes them, but at the core he is weak because of his feeling of fear. Fear is his strongest motivation and this is why he is always suspicious. The only things he can see around him are conspiracies and he feels always surrounded by enemies. Fanatics regard their actions as a way to protect the souls of others and think it is better to have people suffering shortly during their earthly existence than have them suffering for eternity. They think they act for God and do everything for the glory of God.

An important difference between a fanatic and a free thinker is that a fanatic teaches people what to think, while a free thinker teaches people *how* to think.

A human being can not be a fanatic in relation to God, he is only a fanatic compared to other people and he thinks of other people as a barrier between him and God. Fanaticism has nothing in common with religion although often it emerges from religion. God is, so to speak, hidden within the frame, the structure of fanaticism. In this way pathological people exist, and they themselves are not ill, but they spread the seeds of the illness of fanaticism; fanaticism grows well in the ground named religion. A fanatic always needs an enemy. The system of dogmatic formulas on which fanaticism is founded, is always described in human relationships and not in relation to God.

Fanatics of some forms of orthodoxy seek power and not the truth. The truth cannot just be given to man, it is not possible to receive it in a passive way; it is a task without end. The appeal of some systems that are propagated by fanatics is that they promise the truth as a reward when man behaves correctly and conforms to the laws. Truth in this case is very limited and put in universal phrases and clichés. A person within this kind of dogmatic system does not need to live in insecurity or go in search for the truth. The spiritual life of mankind however is freedom and not just a certain form of freedom.

Fanatics are mostly loyal to power and at the same time they don't accept any authority above themselves because they regard themselves as the authorities, and the examples of the only true faith and true religion. A fanatic identifies himself with moral behaviour and is not interested at all in the truth as this can lead him out of the vicious circle of egocentrism. A fanatic egocentric person often tends towards an ascetic way of life and he is not capable of rising above an idea that pretends to be the only way to the truth.

Love for thinking and knowledge is at the same time love for criticism. It is also the love for the development of a dialogue and new thoughts even when they are opposed to somebody's own heritage.

When you do not think for yourself, you don't use your own human potential. The basis of thinking is the recognition of possibilities and impossibilities. And by applying our reasoning, we can distinguish between these two. By doing so we can build a bridge, like Descartes did during the Renaissance, between knowledge, thinking and religion. In the East certain streams went back to the past, back to fanaticism. Thinking leads to questions about good and bad and putting this question is placing the first step. After this we can, with the unity of Rumi in our mind, examine what people in the East and people in the West have in common. What binds these people in both societies, how much the social structures may differ?

The East claims Rumi for themselves, however he is often not understood there.

Consequently, it is equally wrong to claim Edison for the West. Both brought light to the people, without distinction.

There are two ways of thinking, one for the material, physical world and one for the other world. You need to develop two centres, the heart and the head (reasoning). When your thinking is developed it becomes possible to avoid superstition.

Many mistakes have been made in this field. Rationalism, as such, cannot bring spirituality and in the East often someone with a developed heart is regarded as a person without faults while this person can have at the same time very fanatical thoughts and ideas. The heart develops by applying the rhythms, meditation, darkness and quietness. Thinking has to be developed in action, by travelling and seeing the facts.

Often religions and ideologies pretend to be the only way, the beginning of fanaticism is to claim wisdom exclusively. By travelling you experience how relative this is. When you are in the other world posing a question maybe you are able to hear the echo of an answer

The step from fanaticism to rationalism is a big step, the step from rationalism to spirituality and synchronicity is easier. The suppression of women is one of the biggest forms of superstition. Although there are differences between men and women their qualities are equal. The ones who limit women by putting themselves in the place of God do not only go against the women but also against men, against the community and the growing potential of the whole community. The truth is that the substantial evolution is what is most important and differences of gender do not play any role in this.

The most fundamental solution of the problem lies in the inner vibration of the music. The Daf is a bridge between hearts, outside of geography or history. The rhythm unites the heartbeat of two or more people to become one rhythm with the hearts of thousands. We are invited to reason, but at a certain point the thinking stops. We enter the path of love, the path of the heart. Our hearts speak their own language, a language that makes all other languages useless.

In this way, unity emerges.

> *We have to spread love*
> *Let us fill the cups*
> *Let us change the structure of the world*
> *Let us build a new world*
> *If the door of the tavern should close*
> *Do not let the door of hypocrisy open.*

Shah Nematollah says:

"I open the door to everyone."

A human being should not be tolerant to a thing like intolerance.

Chapter 7: One Letter

When he sits, Sheikh Kamel starts with a short story:

The Persian poet Hafez is one of the most famous mystics. On a certain day he asked his first teacher to teach him. His teacher taught him the first letter of the alphabet, the 'A' or 'Alef'. He asked Hafez to study the Alef and the calligraphy of this letter. Hafez started to study this letter for months. In the end Hafez returned to his teacher and asked him to explain the next letters. The teacher answered him that for a good student it is enough to study just the Alef. The Alef is the symbol of unity. So studying the unity was enough for Hafez. After this Hafez said; "In my heart only the Alef is written, the symbol of my beloved. What can I do? My teacher taught me only this.

"The mystical meaning of the Alef, is 'the beloved', 'the independent'. The Alef is long, tall and straight, the symbol of eternity, unity and purity. Calligraphy is the art of aiming the arrow exactly towards the goal. Calligraphy establishes a good balance between the soul, the rational mind and the body. It is the correct way to write the straight and round movements, it is pure rhythm and vibration. To write in this way develops your inner balance more and more. It has to be done with discipline and harmony. Hafez gives a good explanation of the Alef.

The description of a seeker should be as this little story, told in a poem by Hafez. To learn only one letter is more than enough. It often happened that a teacher gave a similar exercise to one of his students. Of course, this task was not given just to improve the manner of writing of the student, but to invite him to meditate on it and let the meaning penetrate deeper and deeper.

To be oriented to your goal is one of the most important aspects of this path. The universe is filled with beautiful and meaningful events; every day there is all kinds of happenings that draw our attention. However, when somebody is constantly attracted towards something new, he can never be a good seeker. This person remains a wanderer, constantly amazed by the new things, but without any substantial progress. At certain moments a student can be unprepared and unconsciously enter a dangerous situation."

The story of the lady in black

Once there was a woman named Alice who travelled the whole world. On a certain day she entered a town and it struck her that all the women in this town were dressed in black. She asked her guide: "Why are all the women we meet here dressed in black?" In answer to her question her guide proposed that she stays in the town for a while.

Alice agreed and she took a room in the caravanserai. When the evening came, her guide appeared and asked her to join him. They went to an old house and entered. In the hall her guide asked her to wait. He went away and came back after a while to invite her to a room where a number of women had gathered. They were all looking at a door as if something was about to happen. Alice sat down in a corner and waited. The door opened and a very handsome man came into the room. He looked beautiful and at the same time humble and a bit shy. He sat down in front of the group and looked at everybody.

At one moment he turned his attention to Alice and by his special attention she felt that her heart was filled with love for him. She forgot all her travelling plans and everything around her and was just watching him. While she looked at him she thought: "How can I get in contact with him? How can I approach him? I want to show him how much I love him; I want to make plans together with him. Nobody can help me; I am alone in this problem."

She drowned in these thoughts until the meeting was over and everybody left. Alice felt very sad, empty and deserted. She went to the guide and asked: "Can you make an appointment with this man for me; I want to talk with him about several subjects." The real reason she did not mention, but her thoughts kept repeating: 'I want to look at him, I want to follow him, what can I do? This is absolutely the man of my life.'

The guide promised to make an appointment for her and after a short time she met the man. During the meeting Alice was completely fascinated by the man and she let go of every restraint. She said to him: "My name is Alice the traveller. My whole life I have travelled restlessly, as a gypsy. Now I want to stop and stay with you because you are the man of my life.

My whole life I have been in search and my whole life I was expecting you and to be honest I already had abandoned the hope that I would ever find you. I want to know more of you.

Please tell me about yourself, how old are you? What do you do in life? What kind of job do you have? Where do you live? How many students do you have?" The attractive man laughed and asked her to stay for one more night. "Tomorrow I will tell you my decision."

Alice had to accept and she had a restless and sleepless night. The next day again there was a gathering and Alice waited together with her guide. When the door opened the attractive man came in, but this time he was in the company of another man who was even more attractive.

Alice forgot the first man at once as she was totally captured by the beauty of this new man. After the gathering she said to her guide: "Now this is the man of my life, please talk to him and make an appointment for me." So it happened and Alice met the second man and when she saw him she said: "You are the man of my life. I promise that I will stop travelling to be only with you. You are the only one for me, you have totally captured me and I cannot imagine living without you."

The second man listened to her and said: "Rest for one night here, I will talk to my friend about your request; tomorrow I will tell you my decision."

So Alice stayed for one night and the next evening the same happened. Again a more beautiful man came to the stage and again she forgot everything and wanted to be in contact with this new man. Several evenings this went on and at last Alice wanted to surrender to the seventh man.

The seventh man waited until she had told him everything and answered: "I am sorry I cannot stay with you, I have another plan in my life." Alice was shocked and immediately she returned to the sixth man and told him: "You are the one I am in love with and with whom I want to live; what can I do?"

One Letter

The sixth man answered: "Sorry I am no longer available; you will have to find another solution for your problem." This went on with every man she approached until in the end she met the first man again.

There was another gathering and this time the first man was alone. Immediately she confessed to him: "I understand that it was my fault. It was a big mistake. What I have done was very insulting to you, how can I ever ask forgiveness?

I can only tell you that I need you more than ever. Please don't let me go even although I had left you, even though I had put a wall between us. Don't be cruel to me. I have only you in my life, everything revolves around you, and you are the centre of my life. I have made a big mistake, but now it is over. I am changed and I have become mature by the many lessons. Now I understand that it was just illusions. I don't know what happened when I closed the door to you. I love you and you alone."

The first man looked at her for a while and spoke: "Sit down with the other ones; I want to tell you all a story. After this I give you my answer."

The girl and the flower

Once there was a girl who was in love with her flower. Her attention was completely with the flower. One day she entered a garden were many flowers were in bloom.

It was a paradise with thousands and thousands different flowers, a breathtaking play of shapes, colours and perfumes. While she walked among the attractive and fascinating flowers she was with her attention totally with her own flower. She felt so happy with the image of the flower in the corner of her room. She regarded herself as the happiest person in the world because in her opinion she had the most beautiful flower.

After this the first man told: "This story is the example of a true lover, nothing more and nothing less. Compare your own state to the state of this girl, are you determined in your love or are you captured by vagabond desires? Love means to be silent and not to be pretentious. Love means to be true in the moment of an exam.

I will give another example:

The little source and the great lake

Once, two sisters were travelling in a boat on the ocean. Their names were Zahra and Zohreh. During a storm they lost their boat and they were shipwrecked on a remote island. They had lost everything except two small jars. It was a desert like island.

After many walks and investigations the two sisters found a little source containing water of an exceptional quality. They were very happy and every day they went to the source to fill their jars with water. Zahra was accustomed to talking to the source: "O beautiful well, you are the source of my life. My existence revolves around you, I am connected to you; I need you for now and ever. In the mirror of your pureness I look at the sky. The moon appears on your surface, the stars disappear in your chest." And the source flowed quietly with a harmonic and melodic vibration.

Zohreh also went to the source every day. She sat next to the source and looked deeply into the water. Gradually she discovered a secret. She understood that this little source was very deep, much deeper than she ever could imagine. She discovered that it was bottomless. Zohreh became very happy, she became accustomed to the melody and she totally surrendered to it. One night it rained long and heavily on the island. When Zahra and Zohreh went outside the next morning, the desert had changed into a beautiful lake. A lake filled with sweet water. For some time they looked at the lake. It was beautiful. When Zahra saw the lake she was totally captured by it and in a moment she forgot the image of the little source in her mind. The great lake now had her complete attention and admiration. She was overwhelmed by this new reserve of water. She took her jar and went to the lake and she removed her clothes and she went swimming in the lake.

She played and sang and clapped her hands filled with enthusiasm and happiness. The little source in the corner of the desert she had forgotten completely. Time went by and although the lake was big, it was shallow. The warmth of the sun made the lake dry. One day she returned to the little source and she was ashamed. She spoke to herself: "I committed a big sin."

The little source was fresh and sparkling as ever. Zahra filled her jar and said: "O my source, you are the real reason of my existence. My life depends on you, only on you. Do not leave me, without you I cannot exist."

The old source flowed. Zahra felt that the water did not have the same vibration as before. To her hands it did not give the same warmth as it used to do.

Zahra did not know that during the time she was happy with the big lake her sister had been faithful to the little source. Her sister did not have any interest, not for any lake. Zahra did not know that when she was swimming in the big lake her sister sat next to the little source and *meditated on its depth. Zahra also did not know that her sister had got a priceless present as a sign of thankfulness and loyalty. Zahra did not know that her sister one evening, before she went back to her room, had been given a gift of love, a beautiful red pearl."*

The first man stopped talking and after a while he goes on: "Rumi says: "Love gives many exams to lovers, so it becomes clear who the real lovers are and who the pretenders are". And he added; "It is no sign of love when you are attracted to a little source when you are in the middle of a dry desert. Love is to be attracted by this little source, even when the desert is covered with a thousand lakes."

Now the first man said that the gathering was finished. People left and Alice went to the man, expecting an answer to her question. He said: "I have told much and I hope you understood the answer. Now I have another plan."

"What other plan?" Alice asked.

"On the other side of the ocean there is a girl who has been praying to God for a long time, asking him to send a person she can fall in love with. So God is sending me to her."

Alice asked: "But what can be the solution for me?"

He said: "Maybe you first have to pray to God to make you mature enough to distinguish between the vagabonds of your desires and real love. The second step is to pray to God to send somebody who you can truly love, forever."

From that moment Alice started to wear black clothes, like all other women in town. It was a sign of remembrance to love. It's been told that Alice decided to wash all the shadows of her desires in order that her heart would become pure and shining with love."

It is silent for a moment in the chapel, many students sit with their eyes closed.

Hafez says:

"Why would my garden choose another

tree above the cypress?

Is the cypress I planted myself less than

another tree?

I have a cypress in my house

I don't long for another tree."

Chapter 8: Jesus and Barnabas

Usually the students enter the chapel before Sheikh Kamel arrives. However, today he is seated already, surrounded by a small group of students. He has been present at the rehearsals of the music ensemble and they have practised together. When more students enter the chapel the members of the music ensemble also take their seats. Sheikh Kamel drinks his tea. Slowly the chapel becomes silent.

"Today I want to speak about Jesus Christ and a disciple of him who remained unknown for centuries, Barnabas. During the two journeys, some of us made in the last years, we found traces of Jesus and Barnabas in Turkey and Cyprus. By examining the evidence, we found that from a mystical point of view, a new perspective emerges, differing radically from a number of stories we find in the Bible.

Next to Ephesus, in the west part of Turkey, there's a village where Mary, the mother of Jesus, had a prayer house. This village is called *Zan Jan* and generally the name is attributed to the apostle John. This apostle had been there, too. But it is much more plausible that the village is named after Mary because in Farsi Zan Jan means Dear Woman.

For centuries it was not known that Mary's prayer house was there, but in the 19th century a Christian mystic had a dream and found the house. In this time, the same stigmata as Jesus had begun to show on her body.

After investigating this, the Vatican approved this as the place where Mary had a prayer house. The Vatican is now responsible for this place and sends people to take care of it. But why did Mary go to Turkey?

Just before Easter time, Jesus was surrounded by his disciples was preaching in Jerusalem and other villages, while the Romans were on his trail. According to the canonical Gospels he was captured, arrested and crucified by them. There is an apocryphal Gospel attributed to Barnabas, in which a different version of the event is introduced. In that book it is written that the Romans arrested Judas instead of Jesus because of his extraordinary resemblance to his master. Jesus hid himself during this time.

From a mystical point of view this is not regarded as an escape by Jesus. Jesus had to carry out another mission. In the story written in the Bible, we read that Jesus knew what was going to happen.

In every story a seed is hidden; a seed that can be planted in order to let it grow. The story as we commonly know it comes from the theologians. The theologians do not understand the mystical point of view.

When Jesus reappeared, he was recognised by Mary Magdalene and Mary of Nazareth. They decided to move with a small group of people to Ephesus in the west part of Turkey.

In the same region there is a cave. It is called the cave of the 'seven sleepers'. The seven sleepers also originated from this mystery school. The story of the seven sleepers we find in the Quran and it describes the period in which Jesus lived in Turkey. Just like a number of the prophets named in the Bible, the Quran contains many stories of Jesus. During this period in Turkey they were governed and suppressed by the Romans.

Jesus gave to six of his disciples the mission to go, under his protection, to a cave and to meditate there and to ask God for a solution. When they set out to the cave they met on their way a shepherd and his dog. The shepherd completely trusted the six disciples of Jesus and he abandoned everything he had, following them to the cave. He was very trustful and happy. The dog went along with him. Often the dog is presented as a symbol of loyalty because it is very loyal to human beings.

In the cave they sat in a circle and they meditated by concentrating on each other's' heartbeats. Each heartbeat is like a bead and the beads are connected by an invisible string and so the meditation becomes like a lens that produces a fire. The cave became a time capsule, driven by the soul. When a number of souls are connected without the intervention of the ego, this becomes possible. They must have been extraordinarily pure and also gifted with the faith of a dog. They were called the 'seven sleepers' despite the fact that they did not sleep.

In this way the body is able to stop death. It is a sign of the control of the soul over the material world. It was 35 AD that they went into the cave and in 345 AD one of them went to a nearby village in order to buy some food. In the Quran it is written that the seven sleepers stayed for 309 years in a cave. Because the money he wanted to pay with proved to be no longer valid, he realised that he was in another era. Shortly before, in Constantinople, the Emperor Constantine had seen the same dream twice. In this dream he was given the mission to go to Jerusalem in order to search the cross on which Jesus had been crucified. After this he converted himself and the Roman Empire to Christianity.

So, to go back to the time Jesus left Jerusalem, he lived in Ephesus in the west part of Turkey in silence and only surrounded by a small group of disciples.

One of his closest disciples was Barnabas. During the time Jesus was preaching in Jerusalem, Barnabas was already one of his closest disciples. Although not much is known about him. Barnabas tried to live like Jesus, humble, empty and poor. It was Barnabas who wrote in Ephesus the gospel of Jesus.

Barnabas later took this Gospel to the central part of Turkey, to a region named Cappadocia. This region is situated in a dry area filled with hills and mountains. Because this region has several sorts of rocks, due to the influence of the water, wind and heat, a special kind of landscape has emerged. From the surface it is not so evident, but this region has many caves.

Often when people were pursued by the Romans in those days, and they wanted to escape, they fled to this region with its many caves. The systems of caves proved to be very good places of shelter from the Romans. Some of the systems consisted of different layers of caves, up to ten floors, connected by a labyrinth of corridors. Their entrance was often hidden behind a bush or underneath a stone and could not be discovered easily.

The caves were not only used in dangerous situations. In Cappadocia, the climate has hot and dry summers and very cold winters. During the summer the caves were cool and during the winter they provided shelter against the cold. The cattle were stalled in the highest caves. When the Romans approached, the people took shelter in the caves and stayed in contact with each other by the use of pigeons that carried the messages. Barnabas came to this region. The people that lived in this region were Mithraists. Now why is this important?

At the centre of this tradition was Mithra, the symbol and carrier of light originating from the Zoroastrians, the fire worshippers. Let us take a closer look at this very important mystical symbol because in Christianity, and also within the Quran, this symbol is described and used. It is a star with four points."

Sheikh Kamel stands up and makes a drawing of two Dafs, one horizontal, one vertical, intertwined.

"The Daf is a big Persian frame drum, with little metal rings on the inside that is often used by the Sufis. This drawing represents the four dimensions, four surfaces and, by the two circles, seven hundred twenty degrees. The tops are the four mountains and in the middle is the centre of the four dimensions. In the Quran there is the story about Abraham who asked God to give him the experience of the process of creation in his heart.

In the Quran it is written: 'Take four birds and tame them in order that they turn to you and put a part of them on the top of a hill. Call them and they will fly to you with speed.' Within this passage of the Quran, God answers the question of how something can inspire a soul. The mystical answer to this question is: Kon, (be).

During the last century science has discovered that electrons consist of four quarks. The quarks in their turn also consist of four elements. The inner vibration determines the form that manifests in the universe.

The birds represent the particles that move freely in space. When the particles join each other this produces energy like nuclear fusion. The point where the central lines cross each other is important to catch the energy.

All that lives consists of earth, water, fire and air. By a certain combination of these elements and the addition of the inner vibration, life originates. The inner vibration acts like a magnet to iron particles.

There are two sorts of life; the biological life consisting of four elements and the spiritual life that is made out of the four spiritual elements. When you are playing a Daf, you influence the three outer dimensions and the invisible fourth dimension. In this way the holy inspiration rises in oneself. This can only be understood by the heart.

The Mithra sign, in the shape of a cross, is a representation of this. This Mithra symbol we see in the caves of Cappadocia. At one of the smaller temples we see seven holes in the form of keyholes, the middle one representing Ahura Mazda, the God of the Zoroastrians. Mithra is the symbol of photons that emerge from the sun and go to your heart. When your heart is dusty and filthy it is not capable of reflecting the light. The Mithra branch is pure mystical and has the goal to realise the sun within your own heart.

When visiting the caves in Cappadocia often you enter small spaces that were used as temples in ancient times. In contrast to a church or a mosque the temple is a part of nature. These temples were named Mehrabeh. The part of the word, *abeh* resembles the word abbey, or monastery. These small spaces give the visitors a very authentic and natural impression. We find here red-brown images of the Mithra symbol, the swastika[7] and the jar of wine. In the temple there is also the image of a cow being sacrificed; the cow represents nature in this case. The only thing a cow does is chew and chew again, she is strongly attached to the material world and at the same time she is a very powerful animal. The lion, symbolising the heavenly forces, is in combat with the cow. The Mithra mystic kills the lower nature by means of the light. Also the snake, the sword and, of course, the sun, are important images that we find here. Often a niche in the form of a Mehrab is built inside the caves.

Mehrabeh means 'temple of the sun' and in the word Mehr we recognise a resemblance to the word Mithra. Also there are many images of wine and water in the caves and images of the knights Saint George and Saint Theodor who are riding on their horses' fighting the dragon with their lances. Within their hands is the cross ascribed to Christ. Except for the niche of the Mehrabeh, there is only a long stone table. At these tables the scriptures were transcribed by the copyists.

When Barnabas came to this region the people recognised in Jesus the personification of the light and so the Mithra mystics became Christian mystics. Christ is the one that brings them light and warmth. The scriptures were hidden in the jars. From ancient times this region is known for its wine, made from the grapes that are

---

[7] Swastika is an ancient religious symbol for many Eastern religions such as Hinduism, and Buddhism. The Sanskrit word svastikais is often translated to mean "lucky or auspicious object". However, the symbol also has significance in the early Iranian methodology and Mithraism.

grown on the poor soil. From this region, the copied scriptures were hidden in wine jars, and distributed to other countries. It is from this region that the Nag Hammadi scriptures originate. You notice that the wine and the jar often appear in mysticism. The jar holds the secrets. You can even fall into the jar yourself, as well."

Sheikh Kamel laughs and looks at his students with understanding.

"The gospel that Jesus wrote was found later and it has been published. It is known as the Gospel of Barnabas and it can easily be found on the Internet. There has been a French publication of it: on one page showing a copy of the original manuscript and on the adjacent page the translation.

Later Barnabas was sent to Cyprus, accompanied by Paul. On this island, Paul tried in a fiery manner to convert the people to Christianity. The Roman governor did not approve this and he ordered Paul to stop on penalty of torture and exile.

Paul did not stop and Barnabas warned the governor that he would be punished if he arrested Paul. The governor did not want to lose his prestige and continued his actions and thus he lost his eyesight. Barnabas told the governor that he would get his sight back if he allowed them to preach freely on the island. The governor approved and after three days he could see again. The governor also was converted to Christianity and so Cyprus became the first place where Christianity was officially accepted without war. Later, Barnabas asked Lazarus to come to the island to take care of the community. Lazarus is buried in a church in the Greek part of Cyprus. It has become a place of pilgrimage. The tomb of Barnabas is in the Turkish part of Cyprus.

For centuries Cyprus has been a place where different cultures mixed. Archaeological excavations on the island have provided us many traces of Mithraism in the form of pots decorated with lines and circles expressing the laws of the universe in a pictorial way. Older statues show us musicians with harps, flutes and Dafs, there are statues of whirling dancers and many ancient objects are covered with images of vibrations. So the Daf players and whirling Dervishes are thousands of years old, much older than Islam.

From Cyprus, Barnabas also travelled to Jerusalem and Bosra. The Gospel of Barnabas was accepted by the churches of Alexandria until 325 AD. In this year the Nicene gathering was held and here it was concluded that all original Hebrew gospels had to be destroyed. A law was proclaimed that the possession of one of these gospels was punishable by death. 270 different versions of the Bible were rejected and banned, including the Gospel of Barnabas.

However, the followers of Barnabas in the monastery of Bosra in Syria remained loyal to Barnabas and the way he taught. Many stories from the Bible also appear in the Quran, and prophets like Abraham, Moses and Jesus are named and recognised by both. Nevertheless, the story of the crucifixion is not written in the Quran.

It is known that Bosra grew into a centre of mysticism in the centuries after Jesus. It became the centre for the Sufis for more than 1,000 years. The prophet Mohammad was educated in this school despite the fact that in the East it is assumed that he was illiterate before he wrote the Quran. It could well be that he did not know the Arabic language, but Bosra was, in that time, situated in the orthodox Christian region where the Aramaic language was spoken. Later Mohammad refers to the Gospel of Barnabas and not to the four evangelists Matthew, Mark, Luke or John."

Sheikh Kamel pauses for a while to drink from his tea and to let the story settle deeper within his students. He continues:

"A seeker always awaits the coming of Christ in his heart. Love is like a cycle, like the coming and the dying of a flower in the garden. The flower is there only temporarily, but the thorns are always there. The beloved is there only for a short period, but the longing for the beloved is always there. A seeker is like someone who looks at the moon, longing to see its full face. For this goal the seeker must be as if in an observatory and always looking out for this event. When the seeker misses the exact moment, it can take a long time before it happens again. It is exactly like the full moon, it takes place regardless if somebody is looking or not.

A seeker always waits for the coming of Christ because he knows that his coming brings his heart to life. When we speak about the dark ages and the period of revelations, we mean that the visible aspect of the Master is only present for a certain time. When the seeker advances on the path he realises that he was dead before the coming of Christ; of course neither the 'historical' nor 'theological' Jesus is meant here.

Christ will come to help you with your problems and the biggest problem you can have is the problem of love. But Christ knocks only at the door of a house, where there are people who listen.

The present time is a period of great darkness, comparable with a star which is invisible in the sky. This means that Christ is present in the world of today, but he is not recognised. According to the

Sufis there is a big period of darkness and a small period of darkness. The small period of darkness was from 35AD until 70 AD when Jesus Christ was living in the world under the name Emmanuel. He lived in Ephesus, but only very few people knew him. The period of big darkness means that he lives among us, but we are not pure enough to recognise him.

Christ has immense powers and abilities. Yet, he is not able to bring the non-believers to the path. Everybody has to make this choice for himself.

The historical and physical reality of Christ we call Jesus. Christ, however, is always present and when you are an advanced seeker you are like a mirror able to reflect the light. When you are empty you reflect exactly the same light. This is why it is necessary first to know Christ in your own heart. Only after this you are able to recognise him in the outer world.

When Jesus Christ was alive, very many people were not able to recognise him. How would you be able nowadays to distinguish him among millions of people?

So Sufism is much older than Islam and it has its roots in Christian mysticism and Gnosticism. Similarities in all Sufi schools are: the Master is Christ, he gives you the substantial life, he is the winemaker, and the wine is the inner substance. The Master is a fire worshipper. He worships the fire and holds the pure fire within his hand. He pours it into the cup of the student. Everything burns, body, thoughts and images, until only the name of God resounds.

Rumi was taught by his Master Shams and gradually he discovered more and more. First his Master was like a bright star, after this his

Master was like the full moon, like the mountains, the ocean and like the sun. In the end Rumi realised that his Master was everything, even his own essence.

Shams had the same light as Jesus, so Shams also was able to give life. Shams had become nothing, so he was able to reflect the pure light. Rumi discovered the reality of Christ by Shams.

Shams did not change into Christ, but he became empty in order for the universal light to appear.

Hafez writes that a spiritual seeker who has the help of the Holy Spirit is able to do the same as Jesus. Rumi said that Jesus was the first one who was able to receive this Holy Spirit and he adds the mysterious words that everybody who receives this Holy Spirit is the first one to receive it. There is, however, only one who can enable this.

This absolute light we cannot perceive by our ordinary five senses. We need to develop the capacities of the soul to be able to perceive this absolute light and we need to understand that this process is like to 'become a member of the same family'. We need our five ordinary senses to find our way in the material world, but they distract us from the essence. We need to develop our inner substance to be able to penetrate into everything and to be in contact with the essential aspects of all things. You have to use the vibrations to penetrate into everything.

As was said, this takes place step by step, the seeker sees different manifestations of the light, like the starlight, the moonlight and so on, but all are manifestations of the same light.

"When you see in your dream a human being who brings quietness and peace to you, this is the manifestation of the absolute light. This light is the border of creation in the material world. It is the top of the mountain, the top that in reality is situated at the bottom of your heart, and on this top God lives. The soul is coming from the top and returns to this top. While you are seeking you see the moon reflected at the bottom of the well, not in the sky. When you see in your dreams the sun, the moon or the stars you see the expression of this light. And when you meet somebody who gives you peace and quietness this person is, as was said before, the personification of this pure light."

In Cappadocia, we saw in the Mithra caves circles divided in four parts. Christians placed an image of Jesus Christ in the middle of these circles.

The Mithra images show the light that is coming from the sky, from the invisible world. It is the image of a particle of light, the photon. This is called Mithra (fire). The images in the caves date from long before Christianity. When Jesus Christ appeared, the Mithra followers realised that he was the personification of the light. So they accepted him and followed him.

An image of the photon can also be found in the Hagia Sofia in Istanbul. Initially this building was a Mithra temple, later it was converted to a church and after that to a Mosque. Now it is a museum. An image can be seen there of Mary with Jesus as a baby. She holds Jesus against her heart and while she and the Emperor Constantine have halos around their heads Jesus has the Mithra symbol around his head. Maybe it gives the impression of a cross, but it has nothing to do with the cross in Christianity, it is the Mithra sign. The image depicts the dream that the Emperor

Constantine had and which the mystics connect to the seven sleepers in the cave in West Turkey. Another picture shows Jesus as a grown man, the Gospel on his lap, Mary and Mary Magdalene next to him.

Emperor Constantine, ruler of half of the world in those days, kneels at the feet of Jesus, wishing to be only the dust at the feet of Christ. These pictures come from a time when this was an esoteric school, the time before the official Christianity and official Islam came. Many of the Mithra images were destroyed or were painted over when the Christians took over, and the same happened again when the Muslims became the rulers.

In the Quran we find the word Mehrab, and we find the story of Zacharias. Long ago, Zacharias meditated in front of the Mehrab and asked God for a son.

His first son had died, but he still wanted to have a son to teach. At last the archangel Gabriel appears and announces him the birth of a son. His son is John the Baptist who will later initiate Jesus. Zacharias and the coming of John the Baptist are very important within the chain of initiations that started with Adam and that goes on until the present day.

The Mehrab used to be built in the direction of Jerusalem, but after what is called 'the period of 'ignorance' people started to build the Mehrab in the direction of Mecca. The Quran however says: 'Wherever you turn your head, you will find God'.

Istanbul was an important spiritual centre, situated on the border between the East and the West and it is for this reason that also Rumi and his father came to this place.

The full name is Mehrabe which means 'temple of light'. The words abbey (monastery) and ab (water) have something in common and within the Mehrab: you will always find a place with water.

A meditating seeker looked in the dark water and in the mirror of the water he found Mithra or Christ reflected.

In a mysterious way, the role of the woman who brings the water in the Mehrab has disappeared during the ages in Islam.

This is a big bone of contention. In ancient times the role of the woman used to be more important than the role of the man, the woman after all, was the one who gave birth to the spirit. In the present, and certainly in the East, this is a very delicate subject.

In Sufism we are very clear about this; there is no difference between the sexes. Women and men have equal capacities to be the representatives of God on earth and they have equal capacities to develop their substantial qualities. Our soul is sexless so all the differences between the sexes disappear at this level.

Don't forget that when we talk about religions and theology that they are all the products of men. All systems of religion and books, almost all are products of men.

There are, however, facts known about the female masters and their disciples, but this information are known only to very few people. Jesus Christ made no difference between Barnabas and Mary Magdalene.

The Master of Ibn Arabi for instance was a woman, and the master of Shams also was a woman. Much of the rejection or neglect of women has to do with the problems men themselves have with women and the projection of these problems on their relation to God. A lot of these projections come from fear and jealousy. Again, in Sufism there is no difference, the only thing that is important is the substance and on that level every difference vanishes.

A striking example of this is literally depicted within the mystical miniatures, the little sophisticated paintings. In them, there is also no difference between men and women. These miniatures, which certainly come from another source than theology, often depict different scenes happening in the same moment within a perspective that we cannot grasp. Time and space are of no significance in these worlds. They also do not depict any shadow because the shadow only exists in the material world.

A mystical miniature can be made of three parts: in the left, depicted in green colours there is the eternal world. Green is the colour of eternity. In the middle there is the mountain of Qaf and on the right side we find the material world, depicted in yellow colours. The light that emerges from the invisible world is blocked by the mountain of Qaf. The mountain of Qaf blocks our ordinary senses, but it cannot block our extrasensory perception. Within the Master we can perceive this light directly when we have developed our eye for this.

Beneath the mountain the main scene is depicted, represented as the centre with the rest around it. When you look deep within yourself and question if you are a woman or a man, you will find that you are not able to answer this question anymore. Your real self is neither male, nor female. In our human form we have two bodies, a visible and an invisible body. Our physical body is dominated by the laws of cause and effect. All material bodies, including the astral and the energetic body must not be confused with the soul. The substantial human nature is like an endless ocean squeezed together in one drop. We have to travel through the seven layers of the heart in order to arrive at this pearl.

Our material body is, just like the entire visible and tangible universe, a combination of matter and energy. The definitions for this have been given by the physicists and other scientists.

When you dissect the structure of an atom then there will be a moment when you jump into the world of plasma. This plasma however is still not energy. It is the fourth state of matter; these four states are the solid state, the liquid state, the gas state and the plasmatic state.

The last state is sometimes also called the ethereal state. Our physical body consists of cells, molecules and so on. We also have a plasmatic body as well as several magnetic bodies. The metaphysical aspect however, the substance, has nothing to do with all these bodies. In reality we are neither the physical body nor these finer bodies.

When we put the world as we experience it in a scheme, going from denser to finer states; it comprises matter, plasma and energy. The material world that we can perceive with our ordinary senses is called Giti. This world is held within another world, the world of ideas, or 'the world of pure forms': Messal. What is described here is the philosophy as it was taught by Plato. The part about 'the world of ideas' is perhaps hard to imagine for us. Within this world of ideas all concepts, all forms in potential are present. Take for example a triangle: A triangle always must be shaped of three angles and it always has to be 180 degrees. Or, as another example, the law, that three is bigger than one. These laws are universally valid.

You also can take another example: Imagine that you are going to make something, you think about this object first, you visualise it, and you calculate it and so on.

The design, the concept, is coming from the world of Messal, just as all the physical laws. Messal, then, is the gathering place of all blueprints. It is a timeless reality and when someone travels here he knows what has happened in the past as well as what will happen in the future. Without Messal the universe would be so chaotic that it would be impossible to maintain it. Messal also is the world of the archetypes.

The world of Messal in its turn is surrounded by the world of 'Minou'. Messal and 'Minou' are outside of time and space while Giti is under the laws of time and space. Giti is dominated by Messal and Messal is dominated by Minou' All these worlds are dominated by the throne of God.

Your soul is full of capacities, full of potential and full of possibilities. However, not all capacities are realised, the hidden capacities of the soul are enormous. When your heart is connected to Messal and Minou then, for instance, you are able to see the future and the past.

I say it once more: The heart is like a very powerful nuclear plant. At the Soveida point, the energy of all the denser and finer bodies accumulates. A human being is the point of connection between the different worlds because his reality is the soul that comes from the spiritual world and which is captured in the material world, in the body.

Only in Zen and Sufism it is possible to make the quantum leap, at the end of the journey, into the emptiness. And on both paths it is only the teacher who is able to do this.

In the Bible, as well as in the Quran, Christ is called 'absolute light'.

The light, Mithra, is the male aspect of God; Anahita, goddess of the water, is the female aspect of God. Water changes the earth and brings forth life. Within the depth of our heart, at the bottom of the well, there is also the water that is like a mirror reflecting the light back to its source. Within Christianity, Christ is the male aspect of God and the mother Mary is the female aspect of God.

For the Zoroastrians their God Ahura Mazda is without sex and to his sides there are angels. At his right side the first angel is Mithra, the first angel at his left side is Anahita. When we were in Andalusia in Spain we visited the house of a Sheikh.

The Sheikh himself stayed in the shadow when he welcomed his visitors. When the sun was shining, the light was reflected in a pool in front of the spot where the Sheikh was seated. This produced the effect of light upon light, so the Sheikh was hidden behind two curtains of light.

When the light that is coming from the sun is reflected by the water, the light is not the only thing that returns to the sky. Also the water that evaporates goes up to the sky. This is the beautiful story of the angel descending in the well and returning to heaven with the water."

Sheikh Kamel stops, allowing his students to feel the intense depth and glory of this timeless image.

Figure 4 - A painting in Cyprus depicting the mystical pearl below the Jesus' feet

Chapter 9: The Pearl

As soon as he sits down this morning, Sheikh Kamel asks some students to darken the chapel.

He wants to show them something. Some of the students connect the video projector. On the white wall appears the projection of a painting.

The painting originates from Cyprus and was created in the first centuries after the death of Jesus. At the right side of the painting we see Jesus Christ standing; the rest of the painting shows the sea, full of motion. A little brown boat can be seen from which some people are drawing their nets filled with fish from the sea. Beneath the water there is a man, a diver. He looks at Jesus. Beneath Jesus' feet there is a pearl.

"The spiritual traveller", Sheikh Kamel starts his story, "is in the middle of the desert, without any water and surrounded by the ever shifting sands. In the desert he is a two-dimensional being, he can travel in length or in breadth. To be more correct, a human being in the desert, the metaphor for the material world, is in reality a three-dimensional being because he also travels in time. The dimension of time however cannot be felt and for an ordinary human being it is not possible to influence this dimension directly. In the end, the human being living in the middle of the desert feels no longer satisfied with the illusions of the material world and he sets out for his centre, his real substance. He travels the desert until he reaches the sea shore. Before him stretches the wide ocean and he decides to set out on the sea. The surface of the sea gives a whole new experience.

The surface of the water, with its foam and waves, is the border between the world of water and the world of air. The surface is continuously in motion but the experience of making contact with the water provides the seeker a short moment of unity.

It is however very dangerous to stay at the surface. The surface of the ocean appears to be a place which holds all possibilities. It gives you the feeling that you can choose yourself if you want to descend into the depths or float and travel around on the ocean. The ocean is a huge unknown territory and it is very tempting to sail endlessly on it. The danger is in the fact that when you are a drop of water on the surface, the sun can evaporate you within a second and the clouds transport you back to the mountains and desert.

Once, Moses guided his people through the desert in the direction of the Promised Land. One day he went to the top of a mountain to pray and meditate. He trusted his people. While he was absent Sameri (Zimri) tempted the people and they started to worship idols. These people lived at the surface of the ocean and they were attracted by Sameri's promise that they would reach their goal very soon. Now this was very tempting.

The way to the pearl within the depths of the ocean is long and difficult and when somebody promises you the pearl can be reached quickly and easily it is very attractive. Also because these people had not developed their extrasensory perception, they could not distinguish between Moses and Sameri.

The Pearl

When Moses returned he was very disappointed. It took them a further 40 years before they finally entered the Promised Land.

It is important for a seeker to dive into the depths. Below the surface there is quietness. When you remain on the surface you cannot experience this quietness. On the surface there is war, there are discussions, thoughts and events. All your imaginations and thoughts are events happening at the surface and all are just the reflections of your thoughts.

When you dive into your depths, it changes the whole dynamic of your life. In the desert and on the ocean you move in length and breadth and in time. When you dive into the ocean you can move in three dimensions. And when your extrasensory perception has developed you also can travel in the dimension of time. Therefore sometimes it is said that a human being lives in two dimensions, a fish in three dimensions and a seeker in four dimensions.

The seeker dives into the depths of his substantial existence. The water is dark and he dives under the guidance of Jesus. Layer after layer he explores the depths of the ocean wanting to go deeper and deeper.

According to the mystic Hafez, this process continues endlessly. A long and exhausting journey begins for a seeker who seriously follows the path, respecting the discipline and the exercises. The seeker travels for a long time apparently without results.

The seeker wants to find something and time passes by. This is why Hafez proposes to travel in ecstasy, drunk. "When the seeker is in a state of ecstasy he is not conscious of space and time so he travels easier" says Hafez. When you are far from your Master you have to use your cup, so play Daf. Diving into the depths can be compared to baking bread. It has to be heated gradually; it cannot be done by a flash of lightning.

Once there were two friends who were always together. They were pearl divers and they were so closely connected that even their breathing had the same rhythm.

Often they went to the sea to dive for pearls. One of them used to dive with a rope around his belly while the other rested in the boat. The friend, who stayed in the boat, held his breath and by doing so, exactly felt when it was time to pull up his companion.

'Ham dam' in Farsi means 'same breath', 'dam' means 'moment', 'dam be dam' means breath after breath. One moment for a seeker is the same as one breath. When you breathe you transport oxygen to the fire. By doing so, the fire is stirred. There has to be some relation to the fire in the breathing. The breathing has to contain some fire of itself, otherwise the fire does not respond. Sometimes you can feel this when you, in a certain atmosphere or by a certain vibration get warm, while in another atmosphere you feel cold.

Jesus points out the direction for the diver. In the painting it is clearly visible that the diver, the seeker, looks at Jesus. He is not oriented at the pearl but at Jesus. Jesus is the one who can give him a new life. By looking at the shape of his body you can see that this man has done a lot of spiritual exercises.

The pearl lies at the bottom of the ocean, in an oyster. Not all oysters contain a pearl, only the oysters which are just slightly opened can produce a pearl. When the shell is opened too wide the water washes everything out. The oyster has two shells, the two shells represent time and space.

The boat with the fishermen is at the surface of the ocean. They are only interested in the fish they are able to catch, they are occupied with themselves, by their work and by the fish they catch.

This is a very old painting and you can clearly see that behind the image of Jesus is the Mithra sign, the sign of light. The two fingers of the right hand of Jesus are stretched, they represent that he has the capability to give orders in the visible and invisible world."

Attentively, the students listen to Sheikh Kamel. "In this painting Jesus is represented as the master. His own path started long before and the different stages of his mystical life have been depicted by various seekers and artists.

In the city of Conche-en-Ouche, in France's Normandy, there is a series of stained glass windows in the church of St. Foy, representing the mystical life of Jesus Christ. Three windows do not only represent the mystical life of Jesus, they also represent the different stages on the path of substantial development, stages that apply to every seeker. Let's take a closer look at these windows."

One of the students takes the DVD that Sheikh Kamel has made in France. After a few seconds we see the first stained-glass window.

Sheikh Kamel continues his story: "Of course it starts with the creation by God in which God lifts his right hand and gives the order; 'Be'. God is the creator of the universe and preserves it every moment by continuously creating it. In his left hand he holds a bowl with a specifically shaped cross exactly at the place of his heart. A photon of light is at the place of Gods heart. Why has a photon been placed here? From the discoveries of physics we know that every particle of light consists of numerous photons.

Long time before Christianity, the Mithraists used the symbol of the cross with a circle in the middle. It was named 'photon', 'vehicle of light'. God has many such names; 'light of lights', 'light upon light' and so on.

This pure and absolute light, source of the visible and the invisible world, we find here, personified in human form; God sits on a throne, a crown upon his head, placed between red and violet, the two opposite ends of the spectrum of the visible colours.

You see here the manifestation of God in a human form. On his heart a photon has been placed. With his right hand he gives the orders concerning the creation and the maintaining of the world.

From the throne of God a broad ray of light streams downwards to the Holy Virgin. This is a special command. At her other side, the archangel Gabriel appears. He is on the verge of announcing the word of God. Mary, representative of pureness and virginity, kneels and lifts her hand, as if to say; 'Do not come close, don't touch me.' In the movement of her dress it can be seen that she is alarmed by this sudden appearance.

She is depicted in a defensive position. Gabriel, the messenger of God, is depicted in a dynamic shape. In his left hand he holds a sceptre. His right hand seems to move downwards as if it announces something, as if he releases something.

The text says; 'Greetings to Thou, o gracious woman.' There is clearly a triangular shape between God the Father, the Virgin and Gabriel. You see the triangle of the sender, the announcer and the receiver. The three pillars of the room in which the scene takes place are depicted in three colours, another sign of the unit of three. There are white lilies, a symbol of pureness and innocence of the heart. Just like the Virgin Mary. At last, we find when we look closely, two details within the ray of light, representing the essential message. A white dove flies downward and a small child, the little Jesus, holding a rod. The rod represents the chain of initiations. It is by the grace of God that this all takes place. Gabriel directs the dove from the 'land of nothing' to Mary. He is the messenger. The dove is the soul; the dove represents our true self. The soul enters the heart and is hidden in the heart. The inner child is filled with joy.

This picture is the highest representation of a human being. The inner substance of each of us is like a dove, a dove coming from the 'land of nothing' to the closed space of an egg. The egg is our heart and its shell is the ego. In the beginning it is necessary to have the protection of a hard shell so the little bird can grow and develop itself. During the first birth, the physical birth of the body, only the egg comes into existence; the dove is not there – yet. The dove is in 'the land of nothing'.

At the command of God, the dove travels from the 'land of nothing' into the closed space of the egg. The transformation of the egg into a dove demands the intervention of a catalytic agent, the mother bird or the teacher. By means of the process of the inner vibrations the second birth takes place within the closed space of the egg and the dove develops inside. This is the child of the heart. This is the invisible child, the spiritual reality of the seeker. When the dove is developed, it has to be liberated, the shell of the egg has to be broken in order to give the dove its freedom. This is the second intervention of the master: the initiation."

Sheikh Kamel pauses for a few moments to let the students absorb his words. He senses that many of them are surprised by his knowledge of Christian mysticism.

"The next stained-glass window" he continues his story, "shows the initiation. Again God is depicted in the top, seated on a pyramid of light. A lot of rays descend downwards and a big ray of light flows to the ceremony of baptism. With his left hand God holds the universal sphere; with his right hand he gives the orders.

Below him the inner child is within the heart of the man, the heart of Jesus. Jesus kneels down in the stream of light and he is full of submission. Next to him, John the Baptist pours the holy water from his hand to accomplish his mission. This is the image of the baptism as we know it, but how can we understand what is hidden in this event? From the hand of John the Baptist water is being poured, but where does this water come from? It comes from a canal high above. This is the moment in which the soul, under the form of a white dove, liberates itself from the eggshell of the ego and the body. He liberates himself from the cage and spreads his wings. Jesus has surrendered and is full of submission. Saint John looks at the dove; he is able to see how the soul liberates itself during this event. By his heart he is the channel for this initiation, he is the instrument of God.

At the feet of Jesus, two birds are depicted, the swan and the duck. The substantial alchemy transforms the seeker into a duck. The duck is a water bird, it is able to swim, but it can also walk and fly. It is not afraid of the waves and of the turbulent ocean of the material world. Both birds are independent from the weather conditions; they are independent from outer circumstances.

They are the symbol of the Master and the student. The swan represents the Master. The Master bows his head full of compassion. Only half of the Master is visible which indicates that the Master has a hidden side. In fact, the Master has many hidden sides and some of them remain secret, also for the students.

The whole process takes place conform the heart and the inner vibrations. So baptism is an initiation, an initiation by which the soul gets the possibility to become free of the body.

In Cyprus numerous very old pictures of the ceremony of baptism have been preserved. In one of these paintings Jesus is depicted naked which indicates that he has surrendered everything.

In this painting Jesus is also seen standing in water and the water is full of vibrations. Around his feet fish are swimming, another symbol of transformation and the fish are shaped like the water; they adopt the form of the vibrations.

The ceremony of baptism by water existed long before Jesus was baptised. In all the pictures of the baptism, Jesus is depicted with his eyes wide open. It is an old tradition and later Jesus Christ will initiate Barnabas. We know of this event because it is written only in the history of Barnabas and not by the four apostles. Jesus initiated Barnabas by water and this tradition goes back to the times of Moses. Moses asked his Master to accept him as a student and he found his Master at a place where two oceans meet. So, it is a place where two oceans meet; likewise, in the Vedic tradition the initiation by water is a known ceremony.

Esfandiar and Rostam

Once there was a knight who lived in the time of Zoroaster, his name was Esfandiar. 'Esfand' is the name of a seed that you can put in the fire to have a refreshing smell and 'Yar' means 'friend'. Zoroaster had initiated him by water, he had poured the water on the top of his head and then he had brought him back from the water. The result of the initiation was that his body had become invincible, no arrow could harm him. From that moment on he served Zoroaster because every prophet needs a knight.

Mohammad for example had Aly as his knight.

There is always resistance when you set out in a certain direction and you encounter a stream that goes against you. You need to have the protection of a visible person. Zoroaster was always in danger because ignorant people wanted to attack him and that is why he needed a knight. This knight was Esfandiar. He helped Zoroaster and opened many regions for him. When Zoroaster died Esfandiar still was a young man. Gradually, because he was alone and far from his Master, he began to feel proud, after all he was very mighty and powerful and at the same time he operated under the flag of Zoroaster.

One day he went to his father who was the king of Iran in those days. He said to his father that it was time to give him the kingdom because he had become very old. Esfandiar argued that he, by his power, was a better protector of the country. His father, however, was very attached to the throne.

He said to his son; "I give you the keys to the kingdom but there is a robber who lives in a castle and this robber does not want to submit himself to me. Go to this castle and conquer it."

This was a very difficult mission because the castle was built on a rock and the people who lived there were very strong. His father said, "When you conquer this castle I will give you the keys to the kingdom."

Esfandiar agreed and in just one day he returned to tell that the fortress had been conquered. He asked his father for the throne, but his father said; "There is another castle in the hands of the enemy and after you have conquered this castle you can claim the keys to the kingdom."

And so it went on, Esfandiar accomplished mission after mission and his father started to worry. He called on Jamasbe, his most important vizier and adviser. Jamasbe was a clairvoyant and a mystic so the king asked him where to send Esfandiar in order he would not return.

"Send him to Sistan, the place where Rostam lives", was the answer. Rostam was a remarkable and strong knight who lived in the south of Iran, in a region that now belongs to Pakistan. So this time, when Esfandiar returned, his father asked him to travel to the south and capture Rostam. "You do not have to kill him, but you have to bring him to me, his hands tied" said the king.

Esfandiar replied: "You are crazy; nobody is able to tie the hands of Rostam." But his father persisted, so he set out.

When he arrived at the castle, Rostam was very happy to see the son of the king and he welcomed him. But Esfandiar told him: "I do not come to visit you, but with the mission to capture you and to bring you to the king with your hands tied."

Rostam said: "Although you are a knight, I am far more powerful than you."

But Rostam did not know that Esfandiar was invincible and he could not see a single reason to fight him.

Rostam spoke to Zal, his father, who was an advanced mystic and a magi. Zal told him that Esfandiar wanted to fight him, but not to kill him. That Esfandiar planned to throw him from his horse and to bring him to the king so that he could claim the throne. Rostam was sure that he would win this fight. Zal warned him that it would not be as easy as he assumed.

The next day the fight started and Rostam found out that Esfandiar was far more powerful than he had thought. Rostam took his bow and launched a hundred arrows towards Esfandiar but the arrows could not hit the body of Esfandiar.

Esfandiar launched only six arrows and at the end of the day Rostam returned to his castle, badly injured. Later in the evening Esfandiar came and warned Rostam that he would die if he did not surrender.

Zal, the father of Rostam, had three feathers of the Simorg. Zal had been brought up by the Simorg long ago and he was a student of him. Zal was like a small child; 'Zal' means 'white'.

When he was born his hair and eyebrows were white. Zal's father had banned the child from the castle and sent him to the desert. In the desert, the Simorg came to him and took him to his nest on top of the mountain Qaf. There he cared for the child as if it were his own. Zal became very wise and very powerful and he was in connection with the Simorg.

In the end the Simorg sent him back to his father although Zal was reluctant to go back. "I am connected to you" he had said to the Simorg. Still the Simorg sent him back and he gave him three feathers and the message; "Every time you need me, you can recite and throw one of these feathers into the fire. Then I will return to you."

The Pearl

Now Rostam knew he was going to die and he did not know what to do. So he made a big fire and the Simorg appeared. Zal explained to the Simorg that in case of Esfandiar's triumph, great difficulties were to be expected. The Simorg healed the wounds of Rostam and took him to the coast. There he showed him a tree of which one of the branches was split in two.

He said; "Take this branch and make it into an arrow that you launch at Esfandiar tomorrow. The universe will guide this arrow."

The next day Esfandiar was very surprised to see Rostam in such a good condition.

Again Rostam tried to change Esfandiar's mind but Esfandiar wanted to capture him or to kill him. Rostam realised that he had no choice. The fighting started and Rostam launched the arrow that hit the eyes of Esfandiar. After the battle Zal came and told Rostam; "When Esfandiar was initiated by his master he did not trust his master completely. The moment the master poured the water on him, he closed his eyes."

This is the reason why Jesus is depicted with his eyes wide open. There is something within yourself that wants to be protected at all costs and only when you surrender completely, without any protection, you become totally invincible. This is a secret that Esfandiar did not know and that is only known to the Simorg. When you hold something back it means that there is an impurity, a problem.

The branch Rostam used comes from the Gaz tree; from this tree nougat is made; this white substance, a mix of a certain liquid with sugar to which pistachio is added. The Gaz tree is very broad and captures the dust of the desert. Most trees have huge branches and not so many roots, but the roots of the Gaz tree can become 300m long in order to fetch the water from the depths of the desert. It is a huge tree standing solid in the desert and it can grow to be very old. For migratory birds the tree is very important, they make their nests in it.

The Simorg also visits this tree to help the people who live near it. This bird that comes from the mountain of Qaf brings happiness. Rostam made his arrow from this tree. Esfandiar was blinded by his ego and did not see the danger. Only in the last moment he realised what happened and he realised that the cause of his death was not Rostam, neither Zal, nor the Simorg, but his father.

After this long story we return to the three stained-glass windows of Conche-en-Ouche to investigate the third window. It shows another stage in the mystical life of Jesus.

The third stained-glass window portrays Jesus as the winemaker. Jesus is connected here to the wine press. God is high in the clouds, his left hand on the universe, his right hand high to create and guide the world. Clearly the screw thread of the wine press can be seen, and Jesus is in front of it. Thus, you see the winemaker. His head is bowed to the right in compassion, his right hand points at his heart while his left hand points down at what seems to be the result of his alchemical work: a reservoir with grapes. The grapes that by the use of the wine press transform into pure wine.

A large quantity of grapes is needed in order to produce a small quantity of wine. The making of the wine is a hermeneutic and alchemical process. Wine is a liquid that cannot be found in a natural form in the world. Grapes however do exist in a natural way and the teacher is the alchemist who changes the grapes into the pure substance. Between Jesus' feet the wine flows from the reservoir into a jar; this wine is the mystical wine and the symbol of the inner substance of the seeker. In mysticism, the jar in which the wine flows is always placed beneath the feet of the Master: by using the winepress the teacher changes all the aspects of the ego of the seeker into pure substance.

The first part of the transformation is the pressing of the grapes by a heavy press. The press functions by a turning, screwing movement. After this the remains are strongly heated by which a process of distillation, purification and evaporation is started, the next part of the alchemical process. The liquid that is evaporated flows to another jar. It is no ordinary wine that results from this process; this is called firewater. In many countries in the southern part of Europe this firewater is still used for healing purposes. The pressed grapes have to ripen for another forty days in a dark jar, shut off from the outside world.

The symbol of the jar is very ancient. In the Quran, God is represented as a potter who crafts everybody he creates, and into who, after a period, a soul enters. The naked Greek mystic Diogenes lived in a jar. The jar is the vehicle of the soul, the belly of the mother.

In ancient times, the dead used to be buried in a jar, its opening turned towards the sun. Within the graves often may jars were found. The journey of the soul is very long, so the traveller had many jars of wine, one for every layer he had to cross. On the pots and jars that were excavated, beautiful pictures of the vibrations can be found; circles and flowing lines. For rational people it is a riddle why the potter endlessly makes pots, only to destroy them. The mystic knows that the potter does not look at the pot, but to the soul.

Next to the jar on this window the tools of the winemaker can be seen; the funnel, the pickaxe and the awl. The lion, carved in the jar, symbolises the disciples that are taken by Jesus to the wine press. They have God's power. At the right and the left side of the winepress there are onlookers watching the process from the outside. From the left part a man uses a golden cup in order to receive some of this costly liquid. He tries to gain theoretical knowledge, but he does not want to be involved in the process itself.

Jesus himself is part of the wine press. This represents a very deep mystical process. This machine for making wine is an instrument of God that enables the transformation of the disciples. The words in the banner say: 'The sun and God of human beings'. A cherub carries the throne of God. The picture of God in this window is the representation of an image by an artist. In mysticism the student sees the image of his master. It is the expression of unconditional love.

Another example symbolising the mystical process of the student is the grind stone in the mill, changing the seeds into wheat. The seeds are thrown on the upper grind stone and this stone has small holes by which the seeds come between the turning grind stone and the fixed stone. The seeds turn around seven times before they have been ground to wheat. Sand and little stones are separated. The lower grind stone is attached to paddles. And these paddles are driven by water.

The water enters from one side and leaves to the other side. In mysticism 'water' means 'energy', 'inner vibration'. The stony ego of the student is ground to powder. The Master grinds his students to dust. To put it more clearly, the Master has a twofold task. His first task, the teaching, is simple, but his second task, the destruction of the ego of the student, is something that cannot be learnt from a book.

In the year 2005, we made a spiritual journey with a group of students. Travelling is important, because it enables you to verify what you have learned; and to investigate it. When we travel we learn directly from the historical facts. One of those journeys brought us to Turkey.

There we visited, what our guide said, was a psychiatric hospital from ancient times. According to our guide, in the past people who were depressed and mentally ill were treated here. First these people listened to beautiful music and after that they were asked to drink water that 'was a little radioactive'. After this they walked through a long corridor, with water flowing on both sides while through holes in the ceiling the priests were saying holy words. In the end, they came to a circular room where they could rest, water flowing around them again. This was what our guide told us.

At this ruin there was a plate representing the building in the shape that it must have been during the time it was in operation. In its original shape it bore a great resemblance to a nuclear reactor. It was a building in which water was supplied from an underground canal that led to a place where it turned round. We know from scientific research that the turning of water agitates and speeds up the electrons and neutrons of the water. The water takes energy from its surroundings and streams towards the centre. At the same time, the turning of the water produces a force throwing the particles out of the centre. These small particles, charged with energy, come into the heart of the electron where they explode. The human body, and especially the heart, gets by this process charged with energy.

So it seems more obvious that this place was used to restore the vital energy of human beings in ancient times rather than as a mental hospital for people with depression. Thanks to our scientific knowledge we can come to this conclusion from visiting such a place.

These kinds of systems also exist at the tombs of the mystics Shah Nematollah Vali and Hafez in Iran. The water is flowing underground and when you turn around the tomb seven times you feel a special energy. You turn seven times, one time for each chakra of the heart, and you arrive at the door to the parallel world. Also in Chartres in France a similar system was constructed, but due to the cross structure of the building, the energy is divided there.

The circular form amplifies the energy and this is why the Dargah, the meeting places of the Sufis, are constructed in a round shape. The magnetism we are talking about here is on the border of the material and the parallel world.

Paracelsus (1493-1541), the Swiss alchemist, was very interested in healing by water and sound. His conclusions were applied later by the Austrian doctor, Franz Anton Mesmer, the founder of magnetism who later lived in France. He discovered that water, when magnetised, has a healing power. Mesmer cured many people and in France this method is still being used frequently. The animal magnetism, as discovered by Mesmer, always existed, but Mesmer classified the knowledge and shared it with others. Mesmer applied a rational, scientific approach for the progress of the whole of humanity."

Sheikh Kamel closes his eyes, letting the beads of his rosary glide through his fingers. Many students sit with their eyes closed, until he finally leaves the chapel.

Chapter 10: Warnings

"*In the mountains of Iran, there once lived a man who knew a lot about snakes. In his village and the surrounding region everybody recognised him as the man who had the greatest knowledge of snakes. He knew all the types of snakes that lived in that place and, what was more important, he was an expert in curing snakebites. Some types of snakes were not dangerous, but there were other snakes whose bite could be deadly within hours. This man knew all the remedies to snakebites and when somebody had been bitten they came to him. One day this man and his son set out to the mountains in order to take their sheep to new grounds. When they arrived at the first well to drink, it was blocked by a stone.*

The man removed the stone, but he hurt his foot by doing so. After he had taken care of the wound and the animals had drunk they went on. Despite the pain in his foot, they reached the first plateau in the evening. They found a simple shelter and tired as they were, soon they fell asleep. During the night the man was bitten by a snake, but he did not notice it since the snake had bitten him on his already injured foot. The next day they went on again, and the man did not pay attention to his painful foot. When they sat down after some hours he noticed that the pain was spreading in his body. This was the sign of a deadly snakebite and only now he realised what had happened. Immediately he went back to the village, but it was too late. Before he reached the village, he died. Everybody in the village was upset when they heard what had happened and they could not believe that this man, who was an expert in snakes, had died because of a snake bite. The one who knew all the symptoms so well had become the victim."

Sheikh Kamel pauses and looks at his students.

He senses that some of them feel uneasy by this story. He continues. "This can happen to all of us. First there is an accident, after this, blindness. It has nothing to do with intelligence or cleverness. You need to be alert and act immediately when something happens. All the people in the village held this man in high esteem. He was, however, very convinced of himself and this was his weak point."

"The shortest way to go to God is by the heart" is what the mystics say; "Be friends with a person who reminds you of God."

Our brains are composed of several parts, and the vibrations we are exposed to, influence the different parts in different ways. Some vibrations can turn a certain part of our brains from an angel into a devil. There are people who are able to direct and to handle these vibrations and who are capable, by doing so, to alter your mental state. It is not possible that two qualities or two states of the mind function at the same moment. When one is active, others are passive and vice-versa. When a part of your brain is in contact with the pearl deep within yourself, the other part stops and you are free from its influences. When you are in contact with other people, the best way to understand them is to feel and to take notice of the reaction of your heart.

When you have a good feeling in your heart it means that you are in the presence of someone who reminds you of God. This is why it is important to be connected to your heart when you meet somebody.

Again and again the question is; "Does this person bring you to your head or to your mind?"

Disturbance follows when this person brings you to your head. If he takes you to your heart, he brings you peace and quietness. This is not an intellectual connection; it is a connection from heart to heart.

When you visit the tomb of Hafez or the tomb of Baba Taher, you can experience an atmosphere filled with love. Baba Taher was a mystic, a Tar player who lived naked in the mountains. At these tombs love can be felt, the stream of love never stops. The same is the case at the tomb of the mystic Saadi. Even after hundreds of years, the perfume of love can be perceived there, love can be felt. Again the connection to the heart is felt first. Intellectual reasoning can come afterwards.

Jesus and Moses are examples of soldiers of God, they wanted nothing for themselves, but they did everything for God; all their service was true and pure.

On a certain day Moses was fighting with the Pharaoh and the Pharaoh spat at Moses. At that moment Moses stopped fighting. The Pharaoh was surprised and asked Moses why he stopped fighting so suddenly. Moses answered that the spitting had made him angry and that because of his anger he was no longer fighting just for God, but for himself.

Within these soldiers of God there is not a single trace of the ego. Because of this Moses, Jesus and Joseph are called lions of God. This name is not for their capacities, but because of their ability to fight the bad characteristics of their ego. Aly's surname is Asad-Allah, the lion of God and you become a king when you strive to be honest in your deeds and when you truly try to reach your goal."

One of the students asks: "Before, you spoke about the vulnerability when you are attracted to beauty. Why can't we enjoy beauty? This beauty is, in the end, also coming from God."

Sheikh Kamel says: "When someone shows you something ugly, you are not interested. Automatically you let ugliness pass by. In the world of the advertising they know that very well. When advertisers want to capture your attention, they have to attract you with something beautiful. This is why they spend a lot of money and attention to the packaging of something. The content is hidden beneath the wrapping, but our attention is drawn by the outside of the parcel.

This is an example of how the Antichrist can lead you in the wrong direction and attract your attention with beautiful things. Sameri showed the people beautiful things with the purpose of distracting their attention from God. Moses showed them beautiful things with the purpose of leading them to God. Every moment we balance between these two possibilities and every moment we can fall. Beauty itself, however, is coming from God.

When you are fascinated by whatever kind of beauty and you are in the presence of someone with bad intentions, this person can take you wherever he wants. You lose your self-control because you are seduced by something else. When you notice that your attention is drawn by something, that you are fascinated by something or somebody, it is very important to keep the contact with your heart.

The path is very difficult and it is in the same time sharper than a sword and thinner than a hair. This is why I tell you to be in contact with your heart when you are fascinated by something. When your attention is drawn, you identify yourself with the object of your attention and you become blind. You become willing to give everything to possess your object of desire or to find out why it is so attractive for you. And this is much harder when an enemy presents himself as a friend, as a wolf in sheep's clothing.

The very first moment is utterly important. The moment you feel that your attention is being drawn by something or someone. I try to contact you by establishing a canal to your heart. When you are fascinated something goes wrong, because the faculty of fascination is in the mind and not in the heart.

Sometimes, a person tries to impress you with their body language and this can be a sign that you have to be alert. When you feel somebody wants to penetrate into your territory, into your energy, stop immediately. In contrast, the spiritual teacher tries to get in contact by a canal to the heart and when this canal is established he leaves you, he will not stay to capture your attention all the time. Be sensitive to changes within your body and changes in your behaviour.

Don't forget that everything falls under the laws of the cycles. There can be days when the sun shines and you feel happy and connected to your heart. There can also be times you are feeling depressed and apparently without a connection to your heart. Just at the moment you feel happy and strong you think that you are not vulnerable, but just in this very moment you can be captured, for instance by over estimating yourself. You need a mirror by which you continuously watch yourself and be aware when you are under the influence of somebody else.

For instance, it is very easy to lose the contact with yourself by becoming too involved with what your eyes are seeing. When somebody has influenced or dominated you once, it is very easy for them to do this again. It is exactly the same as hypnosis, the first time it takes a while to hypnotise you. After this first session you go home, but the second time even just the glance of the one who had hypnotised you before will be enough to hypnotise you again. Hypnosis targets a certain part of our brain which is outside of our own control. Without noticing it a certain part of the brain is switched of while another part is switched on. To wash the impurities left by this connection may take a long time. However when you are connected to your heart, there are no objections against enjoying beauty. The devil first prepares himself before he comes to you, he will study your behaviour and find out where your weak points are.

Maybe during your work or in other situations you are confronted by people who want to enter in your energy. In these cases it is very important that you repeat your Zekr and try to stay in contact with your heart as closely as possible. In our times there are a lot of people presenting themselves as religious or spiritual leaders, when in fact they are deceivers. Especially for people from the West, who are often idealistic and full of trust, it is dangerous. They often immediately trust someone wearing a turban or beautiful dress. So it is important not to be naive. After you have had an experience with a deceiver you will not be so naive any more. Try to be well aware of these kinds of situations.

Once we were travelling and in a little village to a mosque. The mosque is a place to meditate and to pray and often we did so. Other people left us in peace at such moments.

Warnings

The mosque we wanted to visit here was closed and when we walked in the garden someone approached us saying that their sheikh invited us to pray together.

By accepting you leave the initiative to the other person. Can you feel what kind of subtle plan was behind this?

You can for example be impressed by someone who speaks Farsi and who is able to read the poems of Rumi. In this case, you should know that when you practiced the lessons for a few years, you often know much more than this other person. When we talk to each other we speak about mysticism, however, a lot of people try to turn it into an ideology, an ideology to feed the ego and this is not Sufism.

But even when you are hundred percent certain of the path and you have a teacher, this is no guarantee. Snakes can also be found in water and even close to the pearl there can be snakes. In all layers, in all the stages of the substantial evolution there can be dangers.

Maybe you are uneasy about all this and maybe you think that there is an evil power, a bad plan and I can assure you: yes, there is a bad plan. We like to withdraw to our warm house, surrounded by friends, but when we look at the society we see that the negativity is becoming stronger and stronger. When we want to be of significance for our children and grandchildren we have to start acting and stop waiting and hesitating. In order to do this, first work on your self-confidence.

Often we like to blindly trust somebody or something, but this kind of trust is undeserved. You labour on your trust by experiencing. By being in the world and having experiences you are able to compare and to become convinced of something. When you become convinced by your experiences this provides the right ground for trust.

Sufism is under great pressure in today's world. Because many people are interested in spirituality, the interest in Sufism also grows. Each year Turkey earns millions of dollars from the tourists and seekers who come to visit the tomb of Rumi in Konya. On the other hand, the public practice of Sufism is prohibited by the Turkish authorities. When there is something that appeals to a lot of people also a lot of fraudsters enter into the fray.

Totalitarian regimes, aiming to undermine freedom, abuse the practice of Sufism for their own purposes. For them it is often used as a Trojan horse to penetrate into the Western societies.

Personally, often I am ill at ease when I meet Western people full of trust and with good intentions, who want to involve themselves unprepared and unprotected in Sufism without knowing the exact purpose of a certain branch or Sheikh that they want to relate to.

We need to become knights of unity, knights who take care and guard the castle and prevent it from getting infected by wrong elements. When the guardian can be influenced or he is vulnerable, he is not a good guardian. You need to be warned and you have to pass through these experiences to be able to protect yourselves. I don't say this to upset you, but I say to you again: don't be naive.

We can regard ourselves as knights of unity. As such, we don't go out and convert people. But everybody who wants to listen and participate is more than welcome. We offer the message of Christ, the message of light. Certainly, we want to make firstly known what Sufism is not.

Only after this we can explain what Sufism is. By doing so, everybody who comes to listen is well informed and is able to decide if they want to continue this path. The task of the Master is first to bring the light to the students. After the disciples have realised the light, they are sent out into the world.

Now it is important that you make a decision yourself. Do you avoid this problem, do you ignore it or is your conclusion to fight? You should realise that this problem is spreading like a wildfire around the world and it is nothing less than an attempt to take humanity back to what is called 'the dark middle ages'.

When you decide to fight, it gives you no guarantee that you will win, but it is a different attitude than saying that you can do nothing or that what is happening is 'the will of God'. It is most important to have trust. When a trustful person loses again and again in fact he loses nothing. On the contrary, every time he loses and his trust remains unbroken, he wins. By being in action you ask the attention of God and he will help you when he deems it is necessary.

Esghbaz means 'loser in love'. This name is used for someone who lives alone, has only a few contacts and who keeps pigeons. Pigeons demand a lot of attention. The Esghbaz lives alone, without a family, and is only taking care of his pigeons. He focuses on one dove, a Towghy. The Towghy is a female dove with a black ring around her neck, feathers on her paws, and a tail like a peacock. She has a regal appearance.

Every day the pigeons are set free and high above the houses they fly. The Towghy, however, flies far from home in search of other pigeons and she tries to get their attention. Only late in the evening she comes back, often in the company of other doves. These doves follow her because they have fallen in love with her. The Esghbaz selects the doves that have come and he keeps the best ones. One day there is a competition between the pigeon keepers and the Esghbaz joins in this competition.

However, that day his Towghy does not come home and the Esghbaz is very disappointed. Over the next days the Towghy still does not come home and the Esghbaz becomes depressed and starts to drink and use drugs.

His brother, who comes from far away, tries to bring other thoughts to his mind by suggesting that he must go in search of the Towghy and to buy it back or even steal it back when buying is not possible. The Esghbaz does not want to know about all this and in the end he dies of sadness. His brother had seen the pigeons and he starts to take care of them.

He had learned from Esghbaz's experience and therefore he trains not one but twelve doves. It can be understood that he is more unconcerned about his doves than Esghbaz was about his Towghy. After some time the Towghy came back, she had fallen in love with another dove who had abandoned her after a while. Now she realised that there was no longer a place for her in her former house and she had to leave. As she was used to be taken care of, she did not survive long before she became the prey of a wild cat.

Another story in Sufism is about a small knight who, just armed with a bow and arrow, attacks a huge castle. The bow and the arrow represent the body and the Zekr. The knight is small, but full of trust, full of determination, his ego destroyed. When he launches his arrow, it is guided by God. When we are able to defeat dragons by the light from our heart we have become knights of light, knights of Christ, Knights of unity.

Barnabas was sent to Cyprus by Jesus and he converted the whole island. After him Lazarus came and led the people for more than thirty years. Think of the seven sleepers in the cave, all can be an example for us. It was the mission of Jesus to bring light, not to die on the cross. In every age there has been a conflict between darkness and light. Unexpectedly someone sent by God will come and renew our lives. This will be the end of winter, spring arrives again, and there are flowers and sweet perfume, the perfume of hope and happiness. It is the coming of Christ in your heart."

Figure 5- The tomb of Rumi, Konya, Turkey.

Chapter 11: Rumi and Shams

Rumi: "I am like the shadow of the cypress, I become smaller and smaller as the sun rises."

As usual all the students have gathered again in the small chapel when Sheikh Kamel enters.

After he sits down, he nods to one of his students. She takes her flute and after a few seconds the notes flow from the instrument; calm and meditative the sounds float in the chapel. After about five minutes she stops and there is a moment of silence, making the absence of sound penetrate more deeply in all who are present.

"The sound of the Ney is called 'Nava' in Farsi. The outer sound is called Seda and the inner sound is called Nava. The outer sound is the sound that echoes back, it is empty. The inner sound is filled with nostalgia and longing. Seda only penetrates into our brains; Nava goes much deeper.

It penetrates each one of us in the same way.

Rumi writes: "O, listen to the complaint of the reed."

In the Ney comes the wind, from the Ney comes the fire, the father is the Ney player, the mother is the Ney, the children are the melody.

Everyone who listens to the flute is burning inside. Within the Ney there is no stream of air, but a stream of fire.

The reed pen has seven bends or rings. In this way the different parts are connected to each other. 'Ney haft band' means the seven layers of a human being. You cannot play music with the pen, it can only write. Although the pencil is hollow on the inside it has no holes. Inside the pen there is nothing to be discovered. Seven arrows are launched towards the pencil, arrows of love, longing and separation. It has to emerge from longing and eagerness. It is better to be impatient. The flute is like a mirror in which everyone can find his own melody.

The flute has been cut from its origin; its origin is the land of the Beloved. The melody of the flute can only penetrate into the heart of somebody who is filled with longing.

This person has the same inner state as the Ney. The mystical meaning of Ney is the fireplace. Reed is very sensitive to fire and catches fire very easily. It is the first thing that starts to burn. Love burns the lover just like fire burns the reed. Through the inner canal to our mouth and our nose the air leaves our body. This canal, which comes from the heart, is the inner Ney. When the fireplace is active it produces fire. Love has the capacity to activate the fireplace. The Ney, the reed flute is an extension of the inner Ney. We inhale oxygen and we exhale carbon dioxide. Then we are in love, we exhale fire.

Mog is the name of the priest who takes care of the fire in the temple. This name originates from the word Magi. The Mog serves the fire. When the fireplace works, our inner state changes.

Kharabat means sun temple, but it also means ruin as well. This is a paradox. The fire that we activate is the fire of purification. The Mog keeps the fire pure, without smoke. He is like a magnifying glass lighting the fire. A person in search of God has to long for the Kharabat. The Kharabat is the sun temple of the Magi. God is present in the sun temple. The heart of the Mog is like a fireplace, he breathes fire. The fire burns our ego, step by step. The temple is the place where the Magi gather. This is the place where you can find the light of God. Hafez directs the people to the Kharabat.

There is an immediate relation between love, life, God, fire and light. Every human being is the cause of the connection between the invisible and the visible world. The Kharabat is an observatory capturing distant signals from the universe. When the Magi gather, it has the same function as a radio telescope.

During the gathering, the heart of every participant beats in the same rhythm. This functions as a refined mystical telescope. We are able to receive more when we tune our heartbeat during a gathering. Take the image of the telescope; the telescope is in a certain house. When you are in the house next to it you are not able to receive so much information from the universe. In the Kharabat all hearts are united.

You cannot know the wind, it is only possible to feel the wind or for example to see the branches move. When the leaves and the branches are dancing you know that the wind is blowing.

The state of love for instance can be concluded from the sighing in the night, the flowing tears or the prayers in the morning. The beloved is the one who lightens the fire in the fireplace of our heart. The beloved one is the one who is present in the world. When the beloved is not present, I become victim of my fantasies as I start imagining about God and my relation to him. The seeker loves the sun, the sun resembles the beloved. Within the mirror I see the sun but this does not limit the beloved. In every mirror the beloved manifests just as he should be, for every seeker. In our present state we are not able to know God directly, only through the Master.

Gathered here we are separated by our bodies. Now take the image of water. Water is one and indivisible although it may be poured into different glasses.

A hundred cypresses cast a hundred shadows, but there is only one sun. In the material world, the world we live in daily, there is a great deal of differentiation. At the same time, all these differences resemble the unity. Take the cypress; when we identify ourselves with the shadow we turn our back to the light, when we turn, however, towards the light we leave the shadow behind. It is important to become free of your ego, but this is a hard and difficult process.

One important feature of this process is to learn to be detached. Often when people hear the word 'detached' they think of ascetics and monks, doing long and intense physical and spiritual exercises. However, we can start in our daily life, by making a distinction between several forms of attachment. There are, as we can call them, primal attachments, like our family bonds and our job. Of course, these are temporary and they will pass. A seeker needs to have the inner attitude of a gypsy, a vagabond. Yet, more important than these primary attachments is to liberate myself from the urge to become involved in other people's business, judging others, jealousy and all the varieties of this kind of behaviour. Instead of paying attention to the processes of others, we should focus on ourselves. To return to the example of the cypress, it is my ego that blocks the light. So, it is wrong to judge others. As I mentioned before, this is an individual path and a lesson which may be harmful for you, may be helpful to another person."

Sheikh Kamel looks at his students and pauses for a while to take some tea. Then he starts to explain more about the subject.

"The so-called Western approach to almost everything is rational, unambiguous and aimed at clarity and efficiency. Rationality has a strong link to the western conviction that almost everything can be explained by the law of causality, the law of cause and effect. The mystical Sufi path differs in a radical way from this mere rational approach. Slowly Western scientists and thinkers have started to accept the concept of unity wherein not only the causal law, but also the laws of synchronicity, of series, the law of the cycles etc. take their place.

The path of the Sufi, however, still seems often irrational and mysterious. Instead of being in a place with clear roads and signs, you find yourself in a labyrinth exposed to a lot of possibilities. You have to investigate the possibilities by yourself and you are on your own in finding your way. The question possibly arises why the seeker, apparently on purpose, is placed in a difficult situation. This question demands a fair answer. In this path the giving of a direct answer can be compared to giving a precious stone to a child. When the answer is given to you directly it is impossible for you to appreciate the true value of it.

The value of the ring

A young man once approached the Egyptian Sufi master Dhu'n-Nun and said that the Sufis were wrong and some other things. The Egyptian took a ring from his finger and gave it to him.

"Take this ring to the market and see if you can get a gold coin for it" he said.

No one in the market offered the young man more than a piece of silver for the ring. The young man returned the ring. "Now take it to a real jeweller" said Dhu'n-Nun "and see what he offers".

The jeweller offered a thousand gold pieces for the ring. The young man was astonished. "What you know about the Sufis" Dhu'n-Nun said "is the same as what the people in the bazaar know about jewellery. To estimate the value of precious stones you need to be a jeweller."

The first lesson on the path of Sufism is secrecy. Keep your spirituality and lessons secret. A characteristic feature of the ego we all know is that our ego likes to talk and to boast about interesting topics. In the moments during a conversation that you don't know what you are speaking about, your ego is likely to add its own inventions. To talk little and be silent is an important lesson that novices in the monasteries have received through the ages.

A second reason for keeping your lessons a secret is to avoid jealousy from others. This was what Jacob taught to Joseph. Jacob knew what was going to happen to Joseph and he protected him, making the brothers of Joseph more and more jealous. Even if Jacob had explained it all to the whole family, the brothers would have remained jealous, because Joseph was the youngest brother and had, in their eyes, the least rights. In turn, Joseph accepted all the circumstances like the well and the prison.

He accepted because all these were given by God. He flowed with God's stream and despite all conspiracies God's way took its course. Another example is Rumi; Rumi did not talk directly about his Master. Rumi's most famous book The Masnavi, which translated in English extends to six volumes, is filled with all kinds of stories, comparisons and tales. In reality, the book is all about Rumi and his Master.

The famous love story about Layla and Majnun is another example. The author writes in an indirect way. The Master also speaks in an indirect way, when he speaks about the door he means the wall. When he would like to explain something about a cup he starts by describing everything which is outside the room. And after this he describes everything that is not the cup.

This is the way of negation. All Sufi music starts with the note 'la' and 'la' means 'no'. The seeker has to adjust slowly to this approach. This approach is a way to experience a 'bigger reality' in an irrational, hermeneutical and mysterious way. The 'la' is a big pair of scissors the Master uses when the ego wants to take over.

When you visit Konya, the place where Rumi is buried, a museum has been made of the Tekyeh where the disciples used to receive the teachings in ancient times. The Master is pictured holding a big sword. It symbolises that the Master uses the sword daily to cut the thoughts that come to your head; in the end the Master cuts your head, bringing you completely in your heart.

This picture looks sharp and cruel, but you have to realise that your ego is as a dragon. Not just a dragon, but a multi-headed dragon. The nafs, the bad aspects of our ego, manifest themselves in numerous different ways. When you think you have dealt with one, ten others pop up. Some people are ignorant and think they can control their ego by thinking. But in reality our thinking can be compared to a little rabbit while our ego is like a mighty dragon. The rabbit by itself is not able to defy the dragon. The only thing you can do is be under the shadow of your master. Aggression is one expression of the ego, another form is jealousy. I can be jealous because you possess something that I don't possess, but I can also have something and not want you to have the same thing. By ourselves we are not able to see all the traps the ego sets for us.

The father of Rumi was a unique Sufi in his time. Together with Rumi, he travelled from his hometown in Afghanistan to Damascus. In those days, Damascus was a centre for the Sufis, and this was in the same period that the Sufis from Andalusia came to Damascus, so three streams merged in one. When they reached the gates of Damascus in the evening in order to spend the night there, the guard asked them who they were and what the purpose of their journey was. Rumi's father answered: "We come from God and we travel to God." The gatekeeper went to the Sultan who was in the presence of Sohrevardi. When they heard what had been said, Sohrevardi remarked: "There is only one person in these times who can say something like that." They went out to greet Rumi's father and Rumi. When they entered the city, Rumi and his father were on their horses while the sultan and Sohrevardi walked beside them.

Rumi's father was Rumi's Master; he meant everything to Rumi. After his death, he left Rumi only one book, a book full of important spiritual lessons. Later, Rumi became famous and when he taught his students, the book of his father was always near to him. One day Shams stepped into the gathering and held the book upside down. He was illiterate.

"What is this?" he asked Rumi.

"It is not meant for you" Rumi answered and Shams threw the book into the water. Rumi became very angry, so Shams collected the book from the river and gave it back to him. The book was dry. Rumi was astonished and asked:

"What does this mean?"

"That is not meant for you" Shams answered and from that moment Rumi decided to follow Shams. Shams removed the last obstacle. When Rumi met Shams it was a meeting with his true self. He saw that which he had been looking for all his life. During the years that followed Rumi did not become like Shams, but Shams penetrated deeper and deeper into Rumi.

Sufism is the light in your heart, the only path of the heart. In everything you do in the material world your ego is involved. Even when you try to develop the capacities of your astral or energetic body, still you are busy in the material world. You work with finer matter, yet it is still matter.

According to Rumi, our heart is the centre of our existence. We take the heart just as a pump, but a Sufi takes the heart as a nuclear plant. The heart is the centre of the vital energy and it has a physical and a spiritual side. When the rhythms work upon the heart the Sufis believe that the vital energy starts turning. This also explains the reason why we do not turn our physical body during the ceremonies. When, in ecstasy, your physical body starts to move and turn it does not matter. But it is wrong, to start with turning your physical body. You can compare it to a helicopter when its blades turn; it rises into the sky, but when the blades and the cabin turn, then there is chaos.

The heart has the possibility to divide the four elements within us. It is the centre by which the different universes are connected. The turning that can be compared to the grinding stone of a mill separates the inner substance from the rest. Your heart is like a cup filled with a certain amount of energy. All energy is in the Soveida point, a minuscule point at the bottom of the heart. Within the physical heart it cannot be traced, but within the astral body it is present. You can find the door within your physical heart.

So, when somebody's heart is transplanted it does not have any consequences for the Soveida point. This black point is like a universe and you should remember that all the universes have emerged from black holes. When you concentrate on the Soveida, the light grows and it is important that this point is exposed to the right vibrations. After death this point rests in the astral body. It consists of black light and this is very special because black light is invisible.

This black light is your true self but it has no relation with the colour black. Soveida is black matter and this is the reason why you cannot see it. You cannot see the light of your real self because it is pure light, light without any colour. Only when you have developed yourself and you have experienced it, you can understand it. You can see white because it is made up of seven colours. So when you ask: Who am I? the answer is: You are the black light that is captured in the black point in Soveida.

Rumi says: "By our normal senses we are like bats, active in the darkness and orientated to the sunset." The substantial evolution is orientated to the sunrise.

These two are opposite. When the ordinary five senses would have been enough, it was not necessary to create human beings. The ox and the donkey would have been sufficient in the evolution. The purpose of extra extrasensory perception is to learn to see God. These senses don't develop spontaneously, we have to do exercises. Often these exercises are contrary to what we are used to de doing.

Outer circumstances don't give you an extra advantage or disadvantage, your essence is this light that is captured in this small point. From this point it is possible that a small bird develops into a mighty eagle. This development takes place by playing the rhythms on the Daf. Outer light is not of importance, it does not matter if it is sunny weather or a cloudy day. By the exercises we learn to hear the music in everything. All Sufi Masters are mirrors in which you can see yourself. When two Sufis meet, they reflect each other's light endlessly. The surface of the mirror is an illusion.

Rumi tells the tale of the lion who had to wait a long time for the hare to arrive. The hare was his Master. At last the hare comes to the hungry lion who immediately asks him why he is so late. The hare says that on his way he was attacked and eaten by another hungry lion. Outraged the lion asks where this other lion has gone. The hare answers that this lion is in the well. The lion bends over and sees the reflection of the hare and a lion and angrily he jumps towards his image.

The bottom of the mirror is a confrontation between reality and illusion. Because of your own reflection, you are not able to see the real image. The back surface of the mirror is black.

The journey takes you through many layers and it takes a long time before you reach Soveida. It is like a journey to the moon, the goal is known, but it takes time to get there. When the pure light appears in the world, a mixture of light and matter develops. You are the pure light that became red by the impurity of the matter. Before the colour red there is the invisible infrared. On the other end of the spectrum there's the colour violet which is followed by ultraviolet, a colour we cannot see with our normal eyes.

When Hafez writes: "Last night I heard a subtle conversation between the violet and the red rose", this means far more than just a beautiful part of a poem. It is an example of the use of the hermeneutical language. The violet and the tulip are flowers that don't close their petals at night.

The night Hafez speaks about is the hidden world. The mystics experience the material world as a place where light is absent. Light comes from the spiritual world. The flowers are like the alchemists able to transform the dust into colours and smells.

Your goal, the Soveida point, is known to you, yet its full significance reveals itself when you arrive there. When Rumi speaks about Soveida it has a lot of similarities with the atomic theory of Einstein. Einstein also says that the sun is hidden in a very small point. 800 years before Einstein, Rumi wrote:

> *"The sun, hidden in a tiny part,*
>
> *opened its mouth*
>
> *The earth and the universe are*
>
> *smashed to many pieces*
>
> *When the sun jumps*
>
> *from this hidden corner."*

The sun in a part, which is you. Rumi wrote everything in the hermeneutical language because this knowledge was (and is) very dangerous. Rumi discovered this wisdom and used it for the substantial development. He explains to you who you are. Einstein used this knowledge in the material world and discovered how matter can be transformed to energy.

You seek poverty and emptiness, not power or authority. You can be like the sun while you are a poor Dervish.

Soveida is like the shell of an egg that has to be broken in order to give the bird its freedom. All that we are doing here in the material world has nothing to do with our real self, but only with our intellect and the life that comes from the first birth.

A Sufi sets out on the Path of the Substantial Evolution in order to learn to know his real self and develop the inner light of Soveida. He wants to become a man of light, both his arms spread out like big, multi-coloured wings. The red archangel which is often spoken about in mystical texts represents this pure light, becoming red when it mixes with matter.

All these lessons explain the process so clearly that we now know what our goal is when we make this long journey through the desert. We become light ourselves in order to give light to others. We travel through the whole spectrum of colours, from red to violet and beyond.

Slowly the seeker discovers that the energy of the Master in his heart grows. In the end the heart of the seeker is completely immersed in the vital energy of the Master.

Within the universe all is in motion. Everything turns and in the end the heart of the Master is the centre of the turning of everything.

The Master or the 'Pir' is an old man. He is advanced, mature and experienced. The seed of my soul needs the earth of my body. The Pir indicates a state of development beyond time and 'space. When the soul grows it is as old as God!

This is a paradox. The soul is then without end or beginning. The Pir was already there before the universe was created. The Pir drank from the wine before the vine was planted. The Quran describes God as being without end or beginning and by this the Quran means; the God within yourself. The Pir has become mature; he has become timeless so he is eternally young.

The Pir is not given a personal name in the mystical books and it is told that when the Pir looks at a stone he sees the same as a young person looking into a mirror. The Pir speaks in the hermeneutical language. All things sing to him, it is the language of the birds. Only he is able to understand this language.

Shams says in a poem: "The writer wrote three languages; the first language could be understood by everybody, the second language could only be understood by the writer himself and the third language nobody could understand, and this third one is me."

Hafez says: "I could not read a single letter in the book of my life, but because of the longing for your face I remembered everything. I was totally ignorant."

Mystics like Hafez and Saadi often describe a fourteen year old boy capturing their hearts.

Fourteen is the number of the full moon, the sign of fullness. An advanced seeker knows that his heart started beating because of the Master. The Pir is the cupbearer, the Pir is the winemaker. The gathering, also called Sama, is a big tavern and every seeker is a cup of wine. The wine is drunk by its own substance. The Pir has a rational method to produce the wine, the wine starts to dance and an inner vibration appears.

On the inside of the cup, from which the wine is drunk, there are seven circles. Every circle corresponds to a state of inner development. Every seeker places the image of his Master before his own image. In front of people who are not really interested the Master will be friendly and behave inconspicuously.

In the evening a farmer brought his cow to the stable. Later that evening a lion entered the stable and ate the cow. When the farmer came back later during the night he did not know a lion had entered the stable, so he went to the lion and stroked him in a friendly way, thinking it was his cow. The lion responded in a very friendly way.

The stable in this story represents the body. Rumi warns people not to challenge Shams. It is like challenging a cat, but in reality you provoke a panther.

A dedicated student passes through an alchemical process. This is the goal of the path. It is like transforming lead into gold or carbon into a diamond. Carbon has the same components as a diamond, but it only becomes a diamond after it has been put under a heavy pressure. The heavy pressure is formed by the outer circumstances in the life of the seeker and the process of time.

When the seeker is within the presence of his Master he never knows how long it lasts. At the same time the longing produces a big pressure in the life of the seeker when the Master is absent.

The Masnavi was written by Rumi when Shams had left him and the whole book is the expression of the longing of Rumi for his Master. Today, there is much interest for Rumi.

We can understand it because we ask ourselves the same questions he did. And here we find the answers."

Sheikh Kamel recites:

"You are the walking cypress in my garden

Do not leave without me

You flow in my soul just as my soul flows in my body

Sometimes you bring me to the garden

Rumi and Shams

Sometimes you burn me

Sometimes you bring me to the light which opens my eyes

I became pure as light

My ego is finished '

Your existence is hidden in my soul

Shams is the soul of the whole universe

Last night you were in my heart

I am jealous of your dress because it is so close to you

Oh God, please give Shams the illness of

love so he experiences what I experience

I am like a dry desert

You are the source and the rain cloud

I realised the life after this life

My body is like a bow and as an arrow

I fly away."

Figure 6- The Tomb of Shams Tabrizi, Konya, Turkey

Chapter 12: Aphorisms

Within every story there is a seed of truth. This seed you must try to find.

Nezami: "When a student after three years still says 'Me', the lessons have been a waste of time."

The notebook of a Sufi is a heart, white as snow.

'To be or not to be' is an existential question. 'To be or not to be in love' is a mystical question.

Most people search God for themselves. A Sufi looks for God because of God.

The heart is small, there is on only space for one Beloved.

On this path we cannot have knowledge, only ecstasy.

When the donkey sleeps he does not dream of India. The elephant does. When you are not an elephant you can become one by being in the company of another elephant.

I asked my Master: "What is the way to be saved?"

He answered: "Give me a cup of wine and hide the secrets."

On the path of love everything is necessary but nothing is enough.

The universe is based on the vibrations. The practices in Sufism are based on the vibrations.

The Master is presents in all the hearts.

To be in contact with enlightened souls is only possible when we ourselves are powerful and developed. Enlightened souls dwell on the top of the Mountain while the ordinary souls live at the foot of the mountain.

The person to whom beauty is revealed becomes beautiful. Spiritual love starts like this.

Wisdom is opposite to madness. Madness attracts wisdom.

The essence of existence is one point. By ignorance the multiplicity appears.

It is not enough just to be in love with the Master. We have to learn to see the reality of 'light upon light, to experience it and to be it.

Make friends with a teaching Master, stick to your obligations, use your time in a fruitful way and make silence a virtue.

A seeker never gets a satisfying answer to his questions. Questions come from the ego. A seeker will never be satisfied.

We are not created for the world; the world is created for us.

The world is a caravanserai, people come and go. He who has little luggage travels lightly.

In the end the seeker becomes the goal he is searching for.

For a beginner the path is like a school class. For an advanced seeker the path is like a tavern. For a very advanced seeker the path is like a ruin.

The material world is like a tunnel to the divine world.

The Master is like a magnifying glass, bringing together the rays of the sun and lighting the fire.

A change of one syllable means another universe.

You were in my heart before my body existed. You brought the love from another universe. Love is not attached to me, it came from another universe.

I am the foam upon the ocean and the pearl at its bottom.

Nezami said: "The heart is the composition of the soul and the physical body. God created the visible and the invisible world. He gave it the shape of the heart."

Personal experiences of the seeker on the Path of Substantial Evolution must be kept personal, in order to avoid jealousy.

When you are only one evening with the friend, don't pay attention to the snacks, the drinks and the furniture of the house.

You showed the two worlds to the lover, but he only wanted love.

Hafez: "Love is easy in the beginning, and then the difficulties begin."

When you consider the teacher to be the absolute touchstone, you are not a good student. You have to take care of your problems yourself.

In one of the buildings we saw the life giving water came from the mouth of a snake. When you are looking for life, you will have to experience death.

Hafez first got a smile from the Beloved. After this he sought and worked hard for many years without result. When in the end he stopped in despair the Beloved appeared again. The first meeting, the first special experience is a gift. After this the seeker has to wait and to work hard.

Rumi: "Shams is like an ocean in an oyster."

The first birth takes place by the mother. The second birth takes place by the Master.

Love implies sadness. Sadness is the deeper aspect of love.

Friendliness or unfriendliness, both are good when they come from you.

Nezami: "The five senses are thieves because they steal the substantial aspect of reality."

Usually we are far away from the reality and only interested in empty things.

What we do has nothing to do with ourselves but with the second birth. From red to violet we travel through the seven colours, seven deserts. The colour of the first desert is red.

Aphorisms

Not every sage is a teacher.

Rumi: "The world is built upon imagination." First you understand it, then you feel it and after this you digest it. The Master permits you the experience.

Jesus rides to Jerusalem on a donkey. The animal is very close to Jesus, but it is only interested in the grass. You should have the capacities as well as the dedication. Only to be close to Jesus is not enough. You have to be determined.

You do what the Master asks you to do, the results are not important. The Master provides the results. You only empty the channel, the water pours in by itself.

Set your ego a task or your ego sets you a task.

When you grow and start to move in a certain direction you'll experience more resistance than when you rest in one place.

When you are invited to do something for somebody else this makes your life meaningful.

When you only act for your own profit this cuts you from life in the end.

Somebody who searches, experiences the unity in the appearances. Somebody who does not search only sees the appearances.

You walk the path with a candle. The candle is the religion, the walking is the mysticism.

You cannot dominate the ego; this is only possible under the shadow of the Master.

Do what you are asked to do if you consider yourself a seeker. If not, do not consider yourself as a seeker.

"Within the light of neediness and poorness, consider yourself as dead."

A parrot is able to talk and therefore people put him in a cage. Speaking gives pleasure to their ego, but when he is silent, people release him.

A material being is not eternal, so the love for a material being cannot be eternal. Be in love with somebody who is eternal, he will give you life.

Rumi: "I am not afraid to be ruined by life. Beneath the ruins big treasures can be found."

Be responsible for those near to you, but expect nothing from them.

Rumi: "Three words are the result of my life: I was a youth, I became mature, and I burnt."

The pearl comes from the ocean, but it is more valuable than the ocean. The reason of existence for the ocean is the pearl. Even though, the pearl arrives, in time, when the ocean has been created already.

The lover is totally focused on the Beloved, not on himself.

The best measurement in contact with others is the reaction of your heart.

The path is sharper than a sword and thinner than a hair. First you need to experience, after this you become convinced and after this you have full trust. When you start by being trustful you have a chance of 50% that your trust is grounded. Trust after experience is strong as a mountain.

When the student is under the shadow of the Master it gives a lot of courage. This is the sword you receive to fight the dragon.

Rumi says that the secret is not hidden, but in order to see it you need a special light in your eyes and ears. When this capacity is not developed it is a secret to you.

When the mystics look at an image of Jesus they understand other things than the religious people. Take for example the image on which Jesus is depicted sitting on a donkey. The donkey is only interested in the grass, only in the five outer senses. Jesus looks in another direction than the donkey, he has a different orientation, he rides on the donkey, but he is not leaded by the donkey.

The Quran says: "Wherever you turn your head you will find God." For a Sufi this means that you have to turn in order to find God.

The pearl is created by a small quantity of water. If the oyster wants to swallow all the water of the ocean, it cannot give birth to a pearl.

You cannot destroy the idols yourself, only love can do this.

'Wine' means the rhythms and the mystical music. "Just speak about the wine and not about the mystery of the universe for nobody can solve this. Be happy, be drunk."

The energy of doubt works like a termite from the inside out. Even when I am exposed to situations in which I lose, time after time I will still be victorious when I am determined and without doubt.

Discipline on this path is the system of rhythms, the meditation, and the Zekr and so on. When you start with this you can expect resistance.

Before Jesus was born, John the Baptist already knew him and also the three wise men from the East knew of his coming before he was born. When Jesus lived and preached most people did not know him.

Your goal is personal. When every one of us has the same goal we can travel together, when our goals are different it is of no use to travel together.

Everyone is created for a certain purpose, a goal to which he is drawn by his heart.

The wise man is always one step ahead. This is the difference between Noah and the other people. We are building a ship. Work on the reserve in your soul, this is necessary for the coming generations.

Purification is emptying yourself. After this you are filled with the light of God. You achieve inner peace, and then you are loyal to yourself. Nobody is able to catch a gazelle. Still a gazelle can only be caught by coming into action and running after it.

One practices the Zekr for a certain time in order to reach to the light. Another person maybe has to practise for a much longer time. There is a difference, but both reach their goal. When you do nothing, nothing is achieved.

Somebody wanted to make progress on the spiritual path so he asked Bayazid if he was allowed to wear his clothes. Bayazid: "Even when I give you my skin, it is not enough. For forty years I did many practises and then by accident I stepped into a hole. There I discovered the treasure."

Shah Nematollah Vali: "When you do not have a Beloved, why don't you want to search for one? When you have found your Beloved you have to be happy and dance forever."

Figure 7- The Central Mehrab in Mosque–Cathedral of Córdoba, Spain

Chapter 13: A brief history of Sufism

Sufism: The transformation of lead into gold[8]

The system of spiritual education that develops the hidden capacities of the seeker is called: the Path of Substantial Evolution. It existed long before the coming of Islam. Many seekers have followed the method of this esoteric school in order to find the pearl of their real self. The prophet Mohammad was also one of the disciples of this path.

The most important source for the mystical tradition of self-development before the coming of Islam was the Christian Gnostic temple in Bosra in Syria. In this Gnostic school many seekers were initiated. They were known as the Honafa.

Mohammad was initiated in this Christian mystical temple when he was twelve years old. The masters and the teachers of this temple in Bosra were called Bahira or mystics. Their old mystical teachings rooting in lessons given by Jesus are mentioned in different verses of the Quran. In other words, the Quran placed its signature under this substantial school of Christian mysticism. Certain people continued practicing this discipline even after they were converted to Islam. They were the first followers of Mohammad (As-Hab-e-Soffeh). Because these first followers of the prophet had a

---

[8] *Lecture held at the 3rd Shah Nematollah Vali symposium in Seville, Spain 2004 by Dr. Seyed Mostafa Azmayesh. This chapter contains a small addition to the original lecture in the last part.*

connection with, and a practice based on the Quran this pre-Islamic tradition of substantial evolution took on a Muslim colour. Two hundred years after the foundation of Islam, this discipline came to be known as Sufism.

Sufism points at a spiritual path, derived from and ascribed to the spiritual exercises of the prophet Mohammad. The exercises of this path have led many seekers to a complete spiritual enlightenment and beyond. The Quran describes this path at several places:

"Believers who remember God will be given a light to distinguish the truth from the rest", "the path eventually leads to God and those who are honoured most by God are those who remember him the most."

The First period

In the first period Sufism was known as a mixture of ascetic life and alchemy. The first Sufis were looking for an alchemical process to transform the ordinary nature of people into enlightened beings. This process of conversion was compared to the changing of lead into gold.

So the teachers of this path were regarded as 'gold makers' or alchemists.

The word 'alchemy' is derived from the Arabic word for chemistry 'al-Kimia'. It is known as the art of changing lead into gold. In fact, the first Sufi Masters were chemists and they used chemical expressions like 'filtering', 'distilling', crystallizing', 'merging' and so on, to describe the nature of each step on the spiritual path. A prominent example of these Masters is Jabir Ibn Hayyan, father of the chemistry of today and known in the west by the name 'Geber'.

This period lasted for more than 200 years. The motto of the Sufis was: "Lord, multiply my knowledge."

Elixir

During this period a spiritual alchemist discovered a special method of alchemical transformation. By composing and practicing the rhythms of esoteric music and through the use of seclusion and retreat, they realised the 'powerful elixir' of the substantial transformation.

Khalvat

The tradition of seclusion and retreat originates from the period before Islam. Many ascetics used to go at least once a year to the Zavieh (a secluded place for meditation), to spend their days and nights in isolation. The prophet Mohammad would go to the cave of Hira. He received the first divine revelation in the cave of Hira when he was forty years old. The first founders of the Sufi school firmly kept this tradition of Khalvat (spiritual retreat).

They also sent their students to a retreat once a year for a period of 40 or 120 days. They closed the door of the Zavieh for their disciples in order to open the door of contemplation and enlightenment. In the isolation of the retreat the negative aspects that blocked the progress of the students were eliminated. The perfect concentration and absolute practice of the Zekr and the Fekr (the reminding of God) led the seekers to their real self.

Sufi music

Another part of the esoteric elixir was the mystical music or 'Sama'. The tradition of Sama also existed before Islam. There are many 'sayings' (Revayat) about this historical fact by Muslim historians like Bnkhari.

Second period

Rhythms and poetry

Because of the declarations of four famous free thinkers Faraby, Hojwiri, Abul Khyr and Ibn Sina (Avicenna) concerning the importance of music and rhythm in the spiritual development of human beings, the 3rd and 4th period of the Hegira was a revolutionary period in the history of Sufism. The folk and traditional music used in Sufi gatherings during this period became institutionalized and structured within the substantial school.

This school was based on a rational vision concerning the substantial development of the human being. He also developed further the research of Khalil Ben Ahmad who founded the structure of Persian poetry (Arouz). Ahmad was the first knowledgeable man who discovered the theory of the inner vibration or 'zarb e khafy' and who presented this theory in the form of the syllables of 'bahr e hazaj'. This discovery was further developed by Faraby in his book *Moussigy ol kabir* (The Great Music). The most important thesis of this book is that the musical 'Qowl' (rhythmical recitation) is the carrier of the four elements rhythm, harmony, melody and inner vibration.

During the same period, the first document on Sama and the rituals surrounding it were written by Aly Hojvily Ghaznavy in the second half of the fourth century. In this book *Kashfol mahjoub* he explains in detail all the useful information about the tradition, ritual and culture of the Sama in the Sufi centres.

During the same period another revolution took place in the mystical field. A mystic from the same time as Hojviry, named Abu Said Abul Khyr for the first time applied the inner architecture of the Persian poetry as a musical support to transmit the inner mystical rhythms. After this invention the Sufis started to recite the mystical poems during their gathering in the Khanehgahs (monasteries).

Historically, Abu Said was a contemporary of Avicenna, the father of rationalism in the East. Avicenna, followed and developed the mystical, philosophical and rational thesis of his teacher and Master Faraby concerning the spiritual progress on the Path of the Substantial Evolution. In his most important and famous book *Shafa*, Avicenna divides his philosophy into four areas: existence and the nothingness (voujoud va adam), the knowledge and the way of God (elm ol adyan), self-consciousness (ma'refat on nafs) and mysticism (erfan). In the same book there is a detailed chapter on mathematics, also divided in four parts: geometry, algebra, astronomy and music.

He also wrote two independent books about music: *al-lavaheg* (Complementary) and al-*madkhal fy sana atel mossigy* (Introduction to Musicology). The same subject he developed further in books like *Daneshnameh Aly y'* and *'Annejat*. In his other book, dedicated totally to Mysticism and Sufism; *al esharat vat tanbyhat* Avicenna concludes that the Sufi path only can be followed by practicing seclusion and

Sama, and not by reading and investigation. He declares that: "Endurance, retreat, meditation and Sama in general leads to the disclosure of the divine realms that cannot be perceived by the ordinary senses."

Qawwali and the art of recitation

The conclusion of all the theories that came together and the discoveries made in the 3rd and 4th century informs us that a Sufi musical ceremony consists of two parts: Qawwali and instrumental music. Qawwali is a certain way of reciting the poems by emphasising the 'igha' or syllables.

The word Qawwali means reciting and Qowl means rhythmical sentences. The whole Quran can be considered as a Qowl because of its inner rhythm. At the beginning of many verses is said; "Qoll" – recite. So from this point of view some of the prophets like David were Qawwal.

It is known that during the first years after the birth of Islam people were attracted by the inner resonance of the verses recited by Mohammad. Qawwali is the art of mystical recitation.

Instrumental music as complementary to the recitation is the second part of the Sama. This part is mainly played on percussion instruments like Daf, Tombak, Tabla and Dohol, while the singing of the Ney, the Cither, the Harp and the other instruments complements the 'tan-tan' of the 'Zarb' (Tombak).

Third period

Theological Sufism

During the 5th century all kinds of philosophies were prohibited by the theologian Al-Ghazaly. He writes in books like *Almongaz men azalal, Tahafatol falasefeh* and other books that philosophy consists of 3 branches: materialism, naturalism and metaphysics.

The followers of the first don't trust the will of God, the followers of the second don't believe in the resurrection, and the followers of the third don't believe in the resurrection of the physical body. So his conclusion is that all philosophers are heretics and need to be disposed of.

After Al-Ghazaly, every possibility for the further development of philosophy was stopped in the East, a number of philosophers became Sufis because they accepted Sufism the way Al-Ghazaly had described it. In some of his books, he wrote that Sufism is the only straight road to God and the Sufis are the real seekers for God.

He describes exactly that the difference between Sufism and philosophy is in the fact that philosophers would like to solve the mysteries of the invisible world by the use of their thinking and their mental capacities, but that the Sufis are interested in the development of the hidden capacities of their heart. In his book *Ajaeb-ol-qalb*, quoted by Najmeddin Razy in *Mersad- ol-ebad* he writes: "When God takes over the heart it is flooded by grace, enlightened, opened, and the secret of the Kingdom is revealed."

Even when some Sufi seekers like Sohrevardi in the 6th century tried to separate and save philosophy from theology, the fatwa of Al-Ghazaly continued to forbid the return of rationalism to the East. Nevertheless, after Al-Ghazaly, Sufism lost its original rational character and became mixed with theology. Thus, within its historical development Sufism has taken on a more theological colour. The Sufis less and less use rational explanations about their mystical discoveries and, instead, try to find sayings attributed to prophets and other holy people to support their practices. However, in spite of this they keep on practicing the Sama in the Sufi centres, from Khorasan to Shiraz and from Konya to Cordoba.

Fourth period

New attacks on the Sama

In the 7th century scientific discussions about the influence of music on the human body, led to a theological debate about the permission or prohibition of Sama within Islam. Although dancing and music are not prohibited by the holy Quran the Sufi music and dance was a source of irritation to many fundamentalist theologians and the Muslim world became separated in two camps.

Each camp promotes their own point of view using sayings and Revayat (transmissions) ascribed to the prophet. However, the Revayat are not in agreement and often give opposing or contradictory perspectives. For instance, Muslim historians like Bukhari state that the prophet and his wife Aisha were entertained by dance and music by Ethiopians in a mosque in Medina.

In another Revayat it is said that the Daf players on a certain day received permission from the prophet to play the mystical rhythms. After a while everybody was deeply touched, and the prophet felt deep joy known as vajd. He stood up in this state, took off his coat and tore it into many pieces, distributing it among his companions. Ahmad Tussi, a professor from the 7th century points to this historical moment in his book *Bavareg-o- elma*, when he writes: "When somebody would deny the truth of the Sama is would be the same as denying the messenger of God and thus he is a nonbeliever."

Saadi from Shiraz wrote a lot about the Sama in his books *Golestan*, *Boustan* and *Divan Ashar*. He was a disciple of Sheikh Shahabodin Sohrevardi Zanjani (6th century), author of *Avaref-ol-maaref* in which he writes priceless information about the lessons and the teachings in the Sufi centres. A part of these lessons is about the Sama.

During the same century there lived in Konya, Turkey one of the most famous partisans of the Sama: Mowlana Jalaludin Rumi.

Spreading of the Sama

In general the Sufi centres through the ages were, despite the resistance of fundamentalists and theologians, never without the sound of the recitations and instrumental music. This was mainly due to the positive approach of Al-Ghazaly. In his book *The Alchemy of Happiness* (*Kimiaye saadat*) he wrote more than 100 pages about the necessity of the Sama and the spiritual gatherings. And so the old tradition of the Sama remained and it spread among the Sufi orders. It was also practised in Sufi centres in Andalusia. In the books of famous Sufi Masters like Sheikh Abu Madyan Andalossy, the Sama is considered to be the most important method for the substantial development of the seekers.

The tradition of Sufi Masters of Andalusia went from the West to the East after the journey of Sheikh Mohyedin Andalossy (Ibn Arabi) to Damascus. His teachings had a considerable influence in the countries of the East. A short time after his death there was a new Sufi traveller who took the light of Sufism from Syria to Kerman in the south of Iran.

Shah Nematollah

The Sufi mystic Shah Nematollah Vali (8th century) was a great musician in his time. He introduced many innovations to the music of his time. He also gave a very important place to the art of the recitation of Qawwali and it became the most popular musical gathering in the Sufi Khanehgah. The followers of Nematollah used music as their source of inspiration and as a staircase for the substantial development. Shah Nematollah institutionalised the practice of listening to Qawwali music which took place regularly during his Sufi gatherings.

The importance of Shah Nematollah is his establishment of the 720 rhythms as the staircase for the substantial evolution. He taught these rhythms of the Qawwali to his followers and afterwards sent them out to the four corners of the world to teach the lessons of real Sufism. In his book about mystical poetry, he frequently describes the place of Sama in Sufi gatherings, the role of Qawwali and the mystical rhythms in his teachings. He explains how the divine door suddenly can be opened during the Sama when the student is, under the protection and attention of his Master, in a charkh (whirling). One of the famous contemporaries of Shah

Nematollah was *lesan ol gyb*, Mohammed Hafez of Shiraz. He was a mystic, poet, musician, and Qawwal and he used in a profound way the hermeneutical language to explain the mystical contemplation. According to some sources, Hafez met Shah Nematollah in Yazd and lived four years in Shah's Khanehgah.

Majlessy

The Qawwali and instrumental music in two parts was practiced in Iran as well as in Hindustan (India) for several centuries. But after the total prohibition Sama by Molla Mohammed Taghy Majlessy, during the period of the Safavid Empire, and the general prohibition of Sufi orders by his son Molla Mohammed Bagher Majlessy, the art of Qawwali and the knowledge of the mystical rhythms disappeared for more than 200 years from Iran.

Fifth period

Brief return of Sufism to Iran

At the end of the dynasty of Zand (18th century), the Dervishes began to return to Iran. Seyed Abdulhamid Dakani (India), an advanced Sufi seeker, came to Iran and taught the art of Qawwali and mystical music to several people who were interested like Nur Aly Shah Tabassy, Feyz Aly Shah Tabassy, Moshtag Aly Shah Kermani, Hassan Aly Shah Kabloy and so on.

From an image in the Moaven Tekyeh in Kermanshah, a big piece of tile work in seven colours, clearly we can see the reappearance of Sufism.

The Dervishes lived according to knighthood or Fotowat, far away from any religious display. This tableau of tiles is very interesting because it shows the 'house of sports' (Zourkhaneh) in the historical development of Sufism. In Sufism the word 'Murshid' means 'guide' or 'leader', who points the way for to the seekers and guides them on the path of spiritual evolution. The Sufi Master is called Murshid. Just like in the art of the antique sports (varzesh bastany) and conform the expression of knighthood or Fotowat the teacher of the knights is called Murshid. He is the leader of the knights, the persons who learn to develop their real self and to fight their egos. Both the leader of the knights and the guide of the Sufis are called Murshid, they guide and lead their disciples to the light of Aly.

How does the Murshid guide his students? By the rhythms which are the carrier of the hidden vibrations (zarb-e-khafy) played on the Tombak. This tableau is a great example of the reality of Sufism reappearing in Iran. The path of Fotowat is a mixture of mysticism and knighthood. The Zourkhaneh was already a place for bodybuilding, but after this mixture with Fotowat it became for some time a centre for soul building, a 'soul building house'.

When the Sama in the Khanehgah was prohibited by the theologians, the Sufis chose, in order to avoid confrontation, the way of the Zourkhaneh.

The Zourkhaneh is a cultural centre with specific architecture. The entrance is very low; everybody has to bow his head in order to enter the arena. This shows the first steps on the path to self-awareness, the necessary feeling of humbleness. In the Zourkhaneh, the disciples of Aly follow each other to a circular place in the middle, lower than the other part of the arena, called Gowd, in order to turn around their axis. The Murshid is at the same time a Qawwal. By the rhythms he makes the inner energy of the participants turn and whirl. Whirling is not dancing, it produces a transcendental state. In fact the mixture of knighthood with the Path of the Substantial Evolution was the best way to stay in contact with the tradition of whirling.

Sixth period

A new marriage between Sufism and theology

Upon its return to Iran, Sufism was attacked again. Theologians began criticising all forms of mysticism and they claimed that the mystical path was 'bed at'; a new religious invention, a form of heresy. Following these accusations, Muslim fundamentalists eliminated some Sufi Masters like Masoum Aly Shah, Moshtag Aly Shah and they prohibited others like Mast Aly Shah to stay in Iran.

So the Sufi seekers once more were forced to adapt to these external pressures and 'to turn their hat totally'. They distanced themselves from the important tradition of Tassawo' or Sama and they portrayed Sufism as a complementary aspect of theology. They developed a new formulation of Sufism in which theology takes the first and most important place.

Gradually the followers of Sufism started to forget the significance of Sufism as the way to self-awareness and increasingly they came to believe that a good Sufi had to be more religious than the most religious theologian. The Sama and the musical gatherings were totally abandoned.

Science and Sufism

The attitude we describe in the previous lines still exists and for some followers the resistance to bring music back into the Sufi gatherings is as powerful as a taboo.

But today, in the 21st century, no one can continue to be indifferent to scientific discoveries of our time. These discoveries are often the best measure to accept or to reject something. Today, music is being used in medical centres as one of the best therapeutic methods. Scientists already discuss with great eagerness the secret of the direct influence of each rhythm and the hidden resonance of it, played and recited by the Qawwal, to the inner circulation of the vital energy within the body of the living.

This opening to scientific discoveries enables Sufism to break with a number of taboos. Some taboos already have been broken and others will be in the future.

Scientists are very interested to know how, according to Sheikh Shahabodin Sohrevardi, the spiritual development of a seeker who attends the ceremony of Sama, two times a week for two years, is equal to a seeker who spends a lot of time in seclusion doing thousands of exercises and meditations. Science is also deeply interested in the theories the Sufis have developed about the rhythms and the structures of the mystical poetry. These scientists want to know more about the specific rhythms and their inner vibrations that produce a specific resonance in the electrons of the water molecules within the physical bodies of the attendants of a Sufi ceremony. By this impact the body starts, without the Sufi's will, to move and to whirl. Within this powerful atmosphere of Charkh (whirling) in the Zourkhaneh and the Sama in the

Khanehgah, when the disciples turn around themselves, their hands bring to mind the rotating wings that enable a helicopter to rise.

The scientists would like to know how, under the influence of the rhythms, the chemistry of the brain changes and the mental state of the participators changes from anger and sadness to kindness and joy. This chemical process makes us comprehend that Sufism was presented as the art of the substantial Al Kimia, the changing of lead into gold.

In the 2006, the BBC broadcast a documentary about the consequences of heart transplantations. The character and the personality of people who had been given a new heart often dramatically changed. Somebody who never had interest in music now became a lover of certain kinds of music, somebody who used to be a vegetarian, became a meat eater and so on. The heart, as this documentary showed, has its own memory and the structure of its molecules resembles to a great degree that of the molecules of the brain.

Investigations into near death experiences show us people who, after their death, experienced the situation within the operation room and could describe this when they were recovered. As such, the question arises how it is possible to remember such an experience while one is 'out of the body' and where are these experiences stored?

Within the light of these scientific discoveries the coming generation will be able to better understand the Sufi declarations about love, unity, tolerance and spiritual progress.

Acknowledgements

The author wishes to thank Wil Nooij for editing, Joke Bakker for general coordination, Ilse Beunen for designing the cover, Helmut N. Gabel for achieving last rectifications and special thanks to Hans Hoekendijk for compiling the text.

www.ingramcontent.com/pod-product-compliance
Lightning Source LLC
Chambersburg PA
CBHW032114090426
42743CB00007B/352